Observe the Sons of Ulster Marching Towards the Somme

Frank McGuinness was born in Buncrana, Co. Donegal, and now lives in Dublin and lectures in English at University College Dublin. His plays include: *The Factory Girls* (Abbey Theatre, Dublin, 1982), *Baglady* (Abbey, 1985), *Observe the Sons of Ulster Marching Towards the Somme* (Abbey, 1985; Hampstead Theatre, London, 1986), *Innocence* (Gate Theatre, Dublin, 1986), *Carthaginians* (Abbey, 1988; Hampstead, 1989), *Mary and Lizzie* (RSC, 1989), *The Bread Man* (Gate, 1991), *Someone Who'll Watch Over Me* (Hampstead, West End and Broadway, 1992), *The Bird Sanctuary* (Abbey, 1994), *Mutabilitie* (NT, 1997), *Dolly West's Kitchen* (Abbey, 1999; Old Vic, 2000), *Gates of Gold* (Gate, 2002), and *Speaking Like Magpies* (RSC, 2005), and *There Came a Gypsy Riding* (Almeida, 2007). His translations include Ibsen's *Rosmersholm* (NT, 1987), *Peer Gynt* (Gate, 1988; RSC and international tour, 1994; NT, 2000), Chekhov's *Three Sisters* (Gate and Royal Court, 1990), Lorca's *Yerma* (Abbey, 1987), Brecht's *The Threepenny Opera* (Gate, 1991), *Hedda Gabler* (Roundabout Theatre, Broadway, 1994), *Uncle Vanya* (Field Day production, 1995), *A Doll's House* (Playhouse Theatre, Broadway, 1997), *The Caucasian Chalk Circle* (NT, 1997), Sophocles' *Electra* (Donmar, Broadway, 1998), Ostrovsky's *The Storm* (Almeida, 1998), *The Wild Duck* (Abbey, 2003) and Euripides' *Hecuba* (Donmar, 2004).

FRANK MCGUINNESS

Observe the Sons of Ulster Marching Towards the Somme

faber and faber

FLIP

First published in 1986
by Faber and Faber Limited
Bloomsbury House, 74-77 Great Russell Street,
London WC1B 3DA

Printed in the UK by
CPI Group (UK) Ltd, Croydon, CRO 4YY
All rights reserved

The author wishes to acknowledge the receipt of a bursary from the Irish Arts
Council towards the writing of this play.

A CIP record for this book is available from
the British Library

ISBN 978-0-571-14611-6

14 16 18 20 19 17 15

In memory of Michael Hayes

CHARACTERS

KENNETH PYPER	as an old man
KENNETH PYPER	in his thirties
DAVID CRAIG	in his late twenties
JOHN MILLEN	in his thirties
WILLIAM MOORE	in his thirties
CHRISTOPHER ROULSTON	in his thirties
MARTIN CRAWFORD	in his early twenties
GEORGE ANDERSON	in his thirties
NAT MCILWAINE	in his thirties

Observe the Sons of Ulster Marching Towards the Somme was first performed at the Peacock Theatre, Dublin, in February 1985. The cast was as follows:

KENNETH PYPER, as an old man	Geoff Golden
KENNETH PYPER, as a young man	Bosco Hogan
DAVID CRAIG	Lorcan Cranitch
GEORGE ANDERSON	Oliver Maguire
NAT MCILWAINE	Ian McElhinney
CHRISTOPHER ROULSTON	Tom Hickey
MARTIN CRAWFORD	Michael Ford
WILLIAM MOORE	Mark Lambert
JOHN MILLEN	Niall O'Brien
Director	Patrick Mason
Designer	Frank Hallinan Flood

The play subsequently opened in London at the Hampstead Theatre in July 1986, directed by Michael Attenborough.

[Handwritten at top: Difficult to understand, where and when we are? Opens with monologue.]

PART 1: REMEMBRANCE

Low drumbeat. The ELDER PYPER *wakes.*

PYPER: Again. As always, again. Why does this persist? What
more have we to tell each other? I remember nothing today.
Absolutely nothing.

(*Silence.*)

I do not understand your insistence on my remembrance.
I'm being too mild. I am angry at your demand that I
continue to probe. Were you not there in all your dark
glory? Have you no conception of the horror? Did it not
touch you at all? A passion for horror disgusts me. I have
seen horror. There is nothing to tell you. I am not your
military historian. Do not turn me into an example. There
are sufficient records, consult them. You are the creator,
invent such details as suit your purpose best. Those willing
to talk to you of that day, to remember for your sake, to
forgive you, they invent as freely as they wish. I am not one
of them. I will not talk, I will not listen to you. Invention
gives that slaughter shape. That scale of horror has no
shape, as you in your darkness have no shape save what you
bestow upon those you leave behind. Your actions that day
were not, they are not acceptable. You have no right to
excuse that suffering, parading it for the benefit of others.

(*Silence.*)

I will not apologize for that outburst before you. You know
I am given to sudden fits like that. The shock you gave
never left my system entirely. I still see your ghosts. Very
infrequently. During daylight now. Dear Lord, you are
kind in your smaller mercies. Did you intend that we
should keep seeing ghosts? It was the first sign that your
horrors had shaken us into madness. Some were lucky
enough to suffer your visions immediately. Those I
belonged to, those I have not forgotten, the irreplaceable
ones, they kept their nerve, and they died. I survived. No,

9

[Handwritten at bottom: Conflict is in the man. Conflict in Ulster.]

survival was not my lot. Darkness, for eternity, is not survival.

(*Silence.*)

There is a type of man who invites death upon himself. I thought once this is the stuff heroes are made from. I enlisted in the hope of death. I would be such a man. But mine was not the stuff of heroes. Those with me were heroes because they died without complaint for what they believed in. They taught me, by the very depth of their belief, to believe. To believe in you. What sense could you make of their sacrifice? I at least continued their work in this province. The freedom of faith they fought and died for would be maintained. There would be, and there will be no surrender. The sons of Ulster will rise and lay their enemy low, as they did at the Boyne, as they did at the Somme, against any invader who will trespass on to their homeland. Fenians claim a Cuchullian as their ancestor, but he is ours, for they lay down for centuries and wept in their sorrow, but we took up arms and fought against an ocean. An ocean of blood. His blood is our inheritance. Not theirs. Sinn Fein? Ourselves alone. It is we, the Protestant people, who have always stood alone. We have stood alone and triumphed, for we are God's chosen.

(*Silence.*)

Leave me. Do not possess me. I do not wish to be your chosen.

(*Silence.*)

I'm a fool. A liar. I've learned nothing from you but how to preach in your name. You have never forgiven that I started out wrong. I looked on my family, my traditions, my faith, with greatest cynicism. It is your curse upon me. I have to learn the hard way. After the war, for you, I had to be different again. To be extreme. The world lay in ruins about my feet. I wanted to rebuild it in the image of my fallen companions. I owed them that much. I came back to this country and managed my father's estates. I helped organize the workings of this province. A small role. Nothing of import. Was that also what you decreed? Leave

me. Must I remember? Yes, I remember. I remember
details. I remember the sky was pink, extraordinarily pink.
There were men from Coleraine, talking about salmon
fishing. A good man who wanted to enter the Church gave
me an orange sash. We sang hymns and played football.
That is true, football. Someone said the sky is red today.
David said it's pink. And I looked and I could see again.
I saw the sky in him. I knew he would die, for he was
turning from earth into air.
(*Silence. As the light increases,* PYPER *sees the ghosts appear,*
CRAIG, ROULSTON *and* CRAWFORD)
You have bestowed your parting gift. Welcome. You look
angry, David. Have I hurt you by speaking? I can't
understand your silence. Can you, Roulston, you,
Crawford? I envy your happiness together. But you must
call as and when you wish. This place is yours when you
wish it to be. I want you here. I want you to stay with me.
Where are the others? Is Moore still searching for John
Millen? Will he never believe Millen cannot be found? If he
were found, would he not return here? Moore must stop
searching. It is time to rest. I would rest, but when he frees
you from his darkness, he asks questions, as if he wishes to
remember, but I have forgotten most of it myself. Where is
Anderson? Still attending McIlwaine? I saw that, you
know. Cut in two. Anderson falling on him as if his body
could hold McIlwaine's body together. I looked and saw his
blood was the same colour as my blood. When I saw that
colour, I felt my blood on fire and no water would ever
quench it again. The fire burned through my eyes. You
were right, David. The last battle. I died that day with you.
(*Silence.*)
The house has grown cold. Ulster has grown lonely. We
discourage visitors. Security. Men my age have been
burned in their beds. Fenian cowards. They won't burn me
out with their fire. I have defeated fire before. And you will
always defend me. You will always guard Ulster. I miss
you. Each day that increases. Is that because I'm coming
closer to you. Am I at last leaving earth for air? Tell me.

Give me a sign. Touch me. Why are you silent with me?
Have I said too much? Have I said enough? Tell me.
(*Silence.*)
I want to ask you something. I need your answer before I
turn into air. Answer me why we did it. Why we let
ourselves be led to extermination? In the end, we were not
led, we led ourselves. We claimed we would die for each
other in battle. To fulfil that claim we marched into the
battle that killed us all. That is not loyalty. That is not love.
That is hate. Deepest hate. Hate for one's self. We wished
ourselves to die and in doing so we let others die to satisfy
our blood lust. That lust we inherited. The true curse of
Adam. I was born knowing there was something rotting in
humanity. I tried to preserve that knowledge, David. To
die willingly, to die clutching it, but you defied my death. I
need defiance now, David. Ulster lies in rubble at our feet.
Save it. Save me. Take me out of this war alive. Evil is
come upon us. The temple of the Lord is darkness. He has
ransacked his dwelling. The Protestant gods die. (*Sings:*)
'Fare thee well, Enniskillen, fare thee well for a while, and
when the war is over – '
(PYPER *sees more ghosts rise*, MOORE, MILLEN,
MCILWAINE, ANDERSON)
You are here at last. Your rest begins. Moore, Millen,
Anderson, McIlwaine. I have remarkably fine skin,
Anderson. Remarkably fine for a man. Look, David, I've
cut myself peeling an apple. Kiss it better.
(PYPER *holds his arms to the ghosts*.)
Dance in the deserted temple of the Lord. Dance unto
death before the Lord.
(PYPER *sees the ghost of the* YOUNGER PYPER. *As if
introducing that younger self to the other ghosts, he beckons it
towards them, invitingly*.)
Dance. Dance.

PART 2: INITIATION

A makeshift barracks, bedclothes in heaps along the floor. The
YOUNGER PYPER *has already sorted out some bedclothes. He sits,*
his army kit beside him, peeling an apple. He cuts himself.

PYPER: Damnation. Blood.
> (PYPER *sucks his thumb.* DAVID CRAIG *enters.*)
> Hate the sight of it.
CRAIG: Sorry?
PYPER: What for?
CRAIG: I thought you said something.
PYPER: I did.
CRAIG: To me?
PYPER: No, so don't apologize.
CRAIG: Ah, right.
PYPER: I was talking to my blood.
> (PYPER *shows* CRAIG *his bleeding thumb.*)
> I was telling it I hate the sight of it.
CRAIG: Never pleasant to see from man or beast. Lord, this
> place hasn't much order about it. Do we have to sleep on
> the ground?
PYPER: It's the amount of volunteers from our beloved
> province. They can't keep up with us.
CRAIG: How will they train us all?
PYPER: They won't.
CRAIG: We can take any of these bedclothes?
PYPER: I did.
CRAIG: Right.
> (CRAIG *sorts out some bedclothes, starts to make up some sort of*
> *sleeping space.*)
PYPER: It won't stop for hours now.
CRAIG: It's only a cut, man. You're not in your grave.
PYPER: You're making yours.
CRAIG: What?
PYPER: I could have taken the finger off myself.

13

CRAIG: But you didn't.

PYPER: That's not the point. I could have. And why? For the sake of peeling an apple. I was hungry. I had an apple. I wanted to eat it. I had to peel it. And I almost cut my thumb off. You have to take risks in this life.

CRAIG: You find peeling an apple's a risk?

PYPER: I cut my finger, didn't I?

CRAIG: Thumb.

PYPER: Thumb, finger, it's all the same. Kiss it better, will you?

CRAIG: Get away home out of that.

PYPER: I can't go home. I've signed up. The army has me. Once you're in, there's no getting out.

CRAIG: Well, you'll see a lot more than a bleeding thumb before you're out.

(PYPER *screams*.)

PYPER: Now look what you've done. You've really scared me.

CRAIG: Who the hell are you?

PYPER: Pyper, sir, Kenneth Pyper.

CRAIG: Are you sure, Pyper –

PYPER: Call me Kenneth.

CRAIG: Kenneth, are you a fit man for this life?

PYPER: Yes, sir, I wish to serve, sir.

CRAIG: I'm not sir. I'm the same rank as you. I'm Craig. David Craig.

PYPER: David –

CRAIG: Call me Craig.

PYPER: I prefer sir.

CRAIG: You're a bit of a mocker, aren't you, Pyper?

PYPER: Me, sir?

CRAIG: They'll soon knock that out of you.

PYPER: I sincerely hope so.

CRAIG: So do I.

PYPER: Like a piece of apple?

CRAIG: I've work to do.

PYPER: I can't tempt you?

CRAIG: Get on with your business and stop this foolishness.

PYPER: Have you ever looked at an apple?

14

CRAIG: Yes.

PYPER: What did you see?

CRAIG: An apple.

PYPER: I don't. I see through it.

CRAIG: The skin, you mean?

PYPER: The flesh. The flesh. The flesh.

CRAIG: What about it?

PYPER: Beautiful. Hard. White.

CRAIG: Not if it's rotten.

PYPER: What?

CRAIG: The apple. You know the saying. One bad apple spoils the barrel.

PYPER: You forgot your shirt, son.

(PYPER *leaps off his bed, races to* CRAIG *carrying a shirt.*)

CRAIG: I did not forget my shirt.

PYPER: Yes, you did. Here.

CRAIG: My shirt is here.

PYPER: Then whose is this?

CRAIG: It must be your own.

PYPER: No, not mine. I'm wearing mine.

CRAIG: Take your shirt, take yourself and get out of my sight.

PYPER: You don't want your shirt?

CRAIG: I don't want your shirt.

PYPER: Please yourself.

(CRAIG *begins to undress,* PYPER *watching him intently.*
CRAIG *glares at* PYPER. PYPER *shrugs, turns his back. When*
CRAIG *is undressed,* PYPER *turns rapidly.* CRAIG *starts.*)

CRAIG: Will you for God's sake –

PYPER: You're as scared of me as I am of blood.

CRAIG: I am not scared of you.

PYPER: Then what are you doing here?

CRAIG: My country's at war. I –

PYPER: Did you not join up to die for me?

CRAIG: For you?

PYPER: It'll be good sport.

CRAIG: You're a madman, Pyper.

PYPER: Am I, David?

CRAIG: Well, you're a rare buckcat anyroad.

PYPER: Funny word that.

CRAIG: Buckcat? It's a –

PYPER: No. Rare. Are you rare, David?

CRAIG: When I want to be. Army's no place for rareness though.

PYPER: Why not? It takes all sorts to make an army.

CRAIG: True enough. You never know. We could end up dying for each other.

PYPER: No, we couldn't. I won't anyway.

(PYPER *throws* CRAIG *the shirt*.)

A little gift, don't argue. There's plenty more where they come from. Get into uniform, David. You'll catch your death. Then I'll have to follow suit.

(PYPER *begins to undress.* CRAIG *gets into uniform.* WILLIAM MOORE *and* JOHN MILLEN *enter,* MOORE *punching* MILLEN *forward playfully*.)

MILLEN: You never laid a hand on her.

MOORE: Think what you like.

MILLEN: You wouldn't know where to put it if I wasn't there to tell you.

MOORE: Would I not?

(MILLEN *goes to attack* MOORE. MOORE *dodges by greeting* PYPER *and* CRAIG)

Good morning, chaps. My name is Moore, Willy Moore. This specimen is Millen, John Millen.

CRAIG: Hello.

(CRAIG *goes to shake hands.* PYPER *abruptly intervenes*.)

PYPER: Mr Moore? Mr Millen?

MILLEN: Yes?

PYPER: You know where you are, I take it?

MILLEN: Supposed to be an army barracks.

PYPER: It is such. And why are you here?

MILLEN: Who are you?

PYPER: I asked you why you are here, Mr John Millen. I see I had better tell you. You are here as a volunteer in the army of your king and empire. You are here to train to meet that empire's foe. You are here as a loyal son of Ulster, for the empire's foe is Ulster's foe. You are here to learn, Mr

16

Millen. Learn to defend yourself and your comrades, and while you are here, you will learn to conduct yourself with respect, respect for this army, respect for your position in this army, and respect for all other positions above you. Since there are no ranks beneath you, you will never be at ease again until you leave this army. Do you understand that clearly?

MILLEN: Yes.

PYPER: At ease, man.

(PYPER *salutes and leaves them.* MOORE *and* MILLEN *stare at him. When he is undressed,* PYPER *sits cross-legged on the bedclothes, motionless, ignoring their stare.* MILLEN *and* MOORE *take bedclothes, start to unpack kit.* MILLEN *goes to* CRAIG, *mouths the question,* Who is he?, *nodding at* PYPER. CRAIG *shrugs ignorance.*)

MOORE: You boys just volunteered?

CRAIG: Aye, I have anyway.

MOORE: Where are you from?

CRAIG: Enniskillen. Fermanagh.

MILLEN: Know a family Rushton there?

CRAIG: Can't say I do. Where do they live?

MILLEN: A bit outside your own. Tempo.

CRAIG: Should know them.

MOORE: We're Coleraine men.

CRAIG: None better. I'm Craig. David Craig.

(MOORE *and* CRAIG *shake hands.* MILLEN *goes towards* PYPER.)

PYPER: David's the name, David Craig.

MOORE: That's a funny thing. Two boys with the same name.

CRAIG: His name's Pyper.

MOORE: Then why does he call himself –

PYPER: I have remarkably fine skin, don't I? For a man, remarkably fine.

(CRAIG *and* MOORE *rapidly start getting their beds together.*)

MILLEN: Have you indeed?

(MILLEN *notices the others at work. He does so also.*)

17

PYPER: Quite remarkably fine. Soft. I've never done a day's work in my life.

MOORE: Lucky man. This is a desperate kip to house us in. Will we have to make these up every morning?

MILLEN: Where do you think you are? Home? Have you never made up a makeshift bed in your life?

MOORE: Woman's work. You don't join the army to do woman's work.

PYPER: No, not a single day. I once nearly starved rather than do a day's work. In fact I did starve. You wouldn't think that to look at me, would you?

MILLEN: Indeed you wouldn't. Willy, do you sleep on your left side or right?

MOORE: Why?

MILLEN: Your ma warned me you snored. I'm wondering if I should change places.

MOORE: I don't snore.

MILLEN: How do you know?

MOORE: I know.

MILLEN: How could anyone know if they snored?

MOORE: My ma never told me I snored. How come she tells you?

PYPER: I remember that time in France.

CRAIG: What?

PYPER: In France. I nearly starved there.

CRAIG: You've been there?

MOORE: When were you there?

MILLEN: What's it like?

PYPER: That time I thought my end had come. Well-deserved bad end. Absolutely friendless. It was a Friday. I hadn't eaten for two weeks or so. I kept seeing things. Maybe they were there. I felt miles away from everybody. I thought I was dying. Not just in the way we're all dying, but suddenly and unprepared. I thought I was growing wings. But I made a vow I wouldn't die. I vowed that if I survived, I would never go back to France. If I did go back, I asked that I be struck blind. I made a covenant, and I survived.

18

MOORE: You had no money at all or people to pull you through?

PYPER: None.

MILLEN: How did you make it home from France without money?

PYPER: Remember I thought I was growing wings? Well, I flew.

MOORE: Can I ask you something?

PYPER: Anything.

MOORE: What's a rare boyo like you doing in an army?

PYPER: What's a rare boyo like you doing in an army?

MOORE: If I'm rare, what does that make you?

PYPER: Cigarette?

MOORE: If you have one to spare.

PYPER: I don't smoke.

MILLEN: Is this a barracks or an asylum?

(PYPER *begins to whoop*.)

PYPER: Sorry. Don't worry. I'm certified as fit and sane for work as any of you in this army.

(MILLEN *and* MOORE *start to change into uniform.* CRAIG *goes to* PYPER.)

CRAIG: Why did you enlist, Pyper?

PYPER: The name is Kenneth, David.

CRAIG: If you don't want to answer –

PYPER: I enlisted, before I was conscripted, because I'd nothing better to do. No, that's wrong. I'd nothing else to do. I enlisted because I'm dying anyway. I want it over quickly.

CRAIG: I thought you said you were certified fit.

PYPER: Fit for dying. Fit for the grave. Fit for pushing up the daisies. Point proved.

MILLEN: Look, we're going to have to share this place for the training time, Pyper. I've only met you. And I don't like you already. Now I don't care what you're going on about, but no more chat about dying. It'll be looking at us straight in the face soon enough.

PYPER: I'm looking at you straight in the face.

MILLEN: And I don't care much for what I see.

MOORE: We won't argue for the first day, Millen.

MILLEN: That silly chat has no place here. Get enough of it at home. It's more fit coming from crying women. You should have heard them on the stairs this morning. All the superstitions of the day. A red sky in the morning. A warning. We should wait.

MOORE: Where did that saying come from about red skies?

CRAIG: Shepherds.

PYPER: Lambs to the slaughter. Baaaa. OK, Millen. That's French for sky.

CRAIG: It's not.

(*Silence*.)

Ciel. Le ciel. Right?

PYPER: Right. Le ciel rose.

CRAIG: Rose? Pink! Are the skies in France pink?

MOORE: How do you get a pink sky?

MILLEN: Shut your mouth. I often saw a pink sky in Coleraine. So must you.

MOORE: Red maybe, but not pink.

MILLEN: He's blind as a bat anyroad.

MOORE: What's wrong with my eyes?

MILLEN: You've eyes like your granny.

MOORE: That woman could see as well at eighty as she could at twenty.

MILLEN: Did you see the old witch at twenty?

MOORE: Respect that woman's memory.

MILLEN: What have I said against her exactly?

MOORE: You said plenty.

MILLEN: I just said you've eyes like your granny. It's only a saying. Eyes like your granny. Feet like your granny, brains like your granny.

MOORE: That woman could buy and sell you up to her dying day. She had brains in her boots. You've some neck –

MILLEN: Will somebody take that thick horse outside and –

MOORE: I don't need to be taken outside. You might want to be taken outside and taught manners. Have I ever upcasted your family at you?

MILLEN: You have nothing to upcast.

MOORE: I might have plenty, but that's not the point. Have I ever done it?

MILLEN: No.

MOORE: Exactly.

(*Silence*.)

PYPER: To answer your interesting question, David, yes, you get pink skies in France. Not as pink as Coleraine, but still pink.

MILLEN: Give it a rest. I've lived there all my life and I doubt if I've seen one pink sky in the hole.

MOORE: Then why say you did and start this bother?

MILLEN: I was only sticking up for my place.

MOORE: I was only sticking up for my family.

MILLEN: I know. Your granny was a decent old woman.

MOORE: A stupid old bitch and an old rip. Well rid of her. Do you want a cigarette?

MILLEN: Have you enough?

MOORE: Aye.

MILLEN: Right.

MOORE: What about yous boys?

CRAIG: Yes.

MILLEN: Pyper, you'll recall, doesn't smoke.

PYPER: Why not? In celebration?

MOORE: Celebrate what?

PYPER: Peace. Perfect peace.

MOORE: Pay no heed to fights like that.

MILLEN: We have them all the time.

MOORE: Over in a minute.

MILLEN: All forgotten then.

CRAIG: Best way to have fights.

MOORE: Far the best. No grudges.

PYPER: What way do you fight, Craig?

CRAIG: Fight?

PYPER: Fight. Flare up, get it all out, then forget about it. Or are you a grudger?

CRAIG: What makes you ask?

MILLEN: I'd say he's a grudger, that boy.

CRAIG: Why?

21

MOORE: Quiet boy. Still waters run deep, right?

MILLEN: Worst men in a fight.

MOORE: Depends on the fight.

CRAIG: I don't have many fights.

PYPER: You should be at home here.

CRAIG: Give me time.

PYPER: Why spend your time here?

CRAIG: It goes without saying.

PYPER: Say it.

CRAIG: I'm in this for Ulster.

MOORE: Like ourselves.

MILLEN: For the glory of his majesty the king and all his
people.

MOORE: Exactly.

PYPER: For your religion?

CRAIG: Yes.

PYPER: My religion too.

(PYPER *offers* CRAIG *his hand. They shake.*)

MILLEN: You haven't told us yet, Craig, what you're like in a
fight.

CRAIG: Good.

MILLEN: Say so. Strong-looking boy. What are you working at?

CRAIG: The father works a forge. I've been working with him
since I was a child. He's getting no younger. I've taken a
fair share of the heavier work.

MOORE: Sore work that.

MILLEN: When you're used to it, no.

CRAIG: It's a dying skill. I've been at him to get into the motor
business. This pal of mine, he's been learning about
engines and the rest of it outside Belfast. That's where the
future lies. If I'd the money, I'd start up with him. But you
know what it's like working for your own people. Once
they get to a certain age it's all clinging to whatever's there
in their time. Nothing else. Father lives for the place as it
is. That and his greyhounds.

PYPER: Greyhounds?

CRAIG: You know about dogs?

PYPER: We bred, the family bred greyhounds.

MOORE: You wouldn't have struck me as a greyhound man.

PYPER: Beautiful animals. Precise. Lethal.

CRAIG: You should meet the father. My ma often says he should have married a greyhound. He tells us behind her back he married a bitch, so she got her wish.

MILLEN: And you think the blacksmiths have had their day?

CRAIG: Not yet. But soon.

MOORE: How soon?

CRAIG: Twenty years at most.

PYPER: Will there be twenty more years?

MOORE: My heart goes out to the horses.

MILLEN: What?

MOORE: What's going to happen to all the horses?

MILLEN: They'll line them up and run motors over them.

MOORE: Could never kill a horse.

CRAIG: You might soon kill a man.

MOORE: I'll face that as soon as I have to.

CRAIG: Sooner than you think maybe.

(Silence.)

MOORE: I saw a horse being killed once.

PYPER: Why?

MOORE: It was blind.

MILLEN: Who did it?

MOORE: Who else? Brewster, the boss of the factory I worked in. Decent enough if you keep to the right side of him and give him his money's worth, but one sign of slackening and bang, that's you out.

CRAIG: What did you work at?

MOORE: Weaving. Well, I'm a dyer.

MILLEN: For a man half-blind he's a great eye for colour.

MOORE: Funny that, isn't it?

PYPER: No.

MOORE: I always thought it was.

PYPER: And you, Millen?

MILLEN: I'm in the flour mills.

MOORE: He's a baker.

MILLEN: I'm a miller.

23

MOORE: He bakes cakes. Wee buns. He's a pastry chef. That's what his wife calls him when she's getting swanky.

MILLEN: Give it a rest.

MOORE: Give him a skirt and he'll run you up a four-course dinner.

MILLEN: Enough of that.

(MOORE *laughs*.)

CRAIG: And you breed the greyhounds, Kenneth?

PYPER: My family did. Like yours, for pastime.

CRAIG: They don't any more?

PYPER: I don't know.

MILLEN: What do you turn your hand at?

PYPER: I work with stone.

MILLEN: Were you some kind of labourer?

PYPER: You could say that.

MILLEN: Casual work.

PYPER: Yes, a sculptor.

(MOORE *nods*.)

CRAIG: I'd say you're a dangerous man in a fight, Kenneth.

PYPER: Would you, David?

CRAIG: I'd say so.

MOORE: How do you fight, Pyper?

PYPER: Dirty.

MILLEN: I think I hear someone coming.

MOORE: Top brass maybe. Move.

(*They stand to attention by their sleeping spaces with the exception of* PYPER, *who reclines on his*.)

MILLEN: Get yourself covered, Pyper. You'll land yourself in it on your first day.

(PYPER *remains motionless*.)

MOORE: On his own head be it.

(CHRISTOPHER ROULSTON *enters. They relax. He ignores them, gathers bedclothes, starts to unpack kit*.)

You give us all a shock there, boy.

ROULSTON: Shock?

MOORE: We thought you might be top brass.

ROULSTON: I'm not in the habit of lying about my rank.

MOORE: Who accused you of lying?

PYPER: Aren't you speaking to the poor, Christopher? You don't remember me, Roulston? Look hard.

ROULSTON: Pyper?

PYPER: I hoped you'd never forget my face.

CRAIG: Yous two know each other?

MOORE: Must often happen with the amount volunteering.

ROULSTON: We schooled together.

PYPER: But we never shared together. Roulston's best friends were always much younger.

ROULSTON: You've kept your tongue.

PYPER: Are you asking to see it?

ROULSTON: I've heard little of you.

PYPER: Impossible. You've heard everything.

ROULSTON: I try to avoid scandal.

PYPER: Then what do you preach against?

ROULSTON: I no longer preach.

PYPER: That's why you're here?

ROULSTON: Pyper.

CRAIG: I've met you too, Mr Roulston. Well, I've seen you before.

ROULSTON: Where?

CRAIG: Our meeting house. I heard you preach in the kirk.

MOORE: Funny the way paths cross?

MILLEN: I'm Millen, Roulston. John –

ROULSTON: Where did you hear my sermon?

CRAIG: Enniskillen.

ROULSTON: Yes. I remember my few occasions there, Mr –

CRAIG: Craig, David Craig. You certainly shocked us into changing our ways.

ROULSTON: I thought I had tempered that sermon well.

CRAIG: Yes, indeed. You've left off the collar, I take it.

ROULSTON: Yes, I – You thought me too impulsive that day?

CRAIG: Not that, I didn't mean that.

PYPER: What was his subject? Pride?

ROULSTON: A vice you are sick with.

CRAIG: No. Sin.

MOORE: Just sin?

CRAIG: Yes.

25

MOORE: Sorry I missed it.

ROULSTON: Enniskillen is a beautiful town.

CRAIG: It is. Did you manage to get on any of the islands in Lough Erne?

ROULSTON: Unfortunately no, but I have happy memories of your homeplace.

CRAIG: So have I.

ROULSTON: To be expected. To be expected.

PYPER: Well done, Christopher. You're developing a good line in polite clerical nonsense.

(ROULSTON *returns to his unpacking. He takes out a Bible.*)
Sorry, Roulston. Didn't mean it. Don't cry. We have to be big boys here. Tough men on the training ground.

MOORE: Can't wait to get on it.

MILLEN: I'm sure they'll start us with the guns.

CRAIG: Doubt it.

MOORE: Why?

CRAIG: We've just arrived and all that. Might not trust –

MOORE: We're no strangers to guns.

MILLEN: Your mouth is going to get you into trouble.

MOORE: Why? We're all the same here. Even Pyper has admitted he's one of our own kind.

CRAIG: You boys are Carson's men?

MOORE: Too true we are.

CRAIG: The North County Derry Battalion?

MILLEN: That's the one.

CRAIG: Who were yous under?

MILLEN: You're looking at one of them.

MOORE: Best soldier for fifty mile.

MILLEN: Good support in Fermanagh anyway.

CRAIG: Plenty. But it was needed. Every man had his job to do, even if it was only to keep his eyes opened. We have our fair share of Fenian rats. I did a few runs to collect and deliver the wares. We've a couple of vehicles. Was near enough to your part. I could have supplied yous with stuff.

MOORE: The same stuff was badly needed.

CRAIG: Compared to ours, your part is safe enough.

MOORE: No part's safe this weather.

(ROULSTON *has gone to* PYPER.)

ROULSTON: (*Sotto*) Are you going to keep up this attack?

PYPER: Do you want me to?

(ROULSTON *leaves*.)

MOORE: Getting a bit too big for their boots everywhere. Tell him about the pup we had to deal with.

MILLEN: We went out one morning, himself and myself, one Saturday, not that long ago, early-morning training session, near Bushmills.

MOORE: The smoke from a Papist chimney will never darken the skies of Bushmills.

MILLEN: Am I telling the story or you? Gathering near the lodge, first thing we saw, painted on the left wall, would you credit this, a tricolour.

MOORE: A tricolour. Painted on an orange lodge.

MILLEN: Green, white and gold.

MOORE: Green, shite and gold. It wasn't there for long.

PYPER: Go on.

MILLEN: You listening?

PYPER: Every word.

MILLEN: We tracked down the artist. Sixteen years old. Wanted to die for Ireland.

MOORE: The mother a widow woman, decent enough creature for a Papist.

MILLEN: We rounded him out. Her crying not to shoot him, he was only a wain.

MOORE: Did better than shoot him.

PYPER: What?

MILLEN: Battered him down the streets of Coleraine.

MOORE: Shaved every hair off his head.

MILLEN: Cut the backside out of his trousers.

MOORE: Painted his arse green, white and gold.

MILLEN: That cured him of tricolours.

(PYPER *roars with laughter*. MARTIN CRAWFORD *enters. He stops at the pile of bedclothes*.)

CRAWFORD: Is this where we're supposed to be?

CRAIG: What?

27

CRAWFORD: This is where we sleep?

MILLEN: Looks like it, doesn't it?

MOORE: Better grab what's going.

CRAWFORD: Thanks.

MILLEN: Who are you, son?

CRAWFORD: I'm Crawford. Martin Crawford from Derry
Town, sir.

MILLEN: Whereabouts?

CRAWFORD: Foyle Street.

MILLEN: What number?

CRAWFORD: Number 27, sir.

MILLEN: Do you sleep on your right side or your left?

CRAWFORD: Sorry?

MILLEN: Nothing.

(CRAIG *has gone to* PYPER. CRAWFORD *gets bedclothes, tries
to unpack kit and make up a bed at the same time.* MOORE *and*
MILLEN *watch his efforts.*)

CRAIG: So you didn't enjoy France?

PYPER: Didn't I?

CRAIG: You said you nearly starved there.

PYPER: Yes, I'd forgotten that.

CRAIG: What part were you in?

PYPER: Paris, I think.

CRAIG: You don't know?

PYPER: Let me think about it.

MILLEN: You're not making much of a fist with that bed.

CRAWFORD: I'm not.

MILLEN: Might be handier if you tried one thing at a time.

CRAWFORD: Yes.

(MILLEN *takes the bedclothes.*)

MILLEN: Show us them. Watch me.

CRAWFORD: Yes, sir.

CRAIG: What were the women like?

PYPER: French women?

CRAIG: Aye.

PYPER: Whores. Everyone of them. Whores. Wonderful
whores.

MOORE: Go on, Pyper.

28

PYPER: I married one.

MOORE: A French woman?

PYPER: Yes, a whore. A Papist whore. I married her out of curiosity.

ROULSTON: Do we need details of your foul life here?

MOORE: Don't listen if you don't want to.

ROULSTON: There's a fellow here no more than a lad.

MOORE: Crawford?

PYPER: He means himself.

ROULSTON: I mean –

MOORE: Shut your mouth. What were you curious about, Pyper?

PYPER: What they're like when they're naked. Papists.

ROULSTON: Turn your mind away from this evil, young man.

CRAWFORD: I've enough to do without listening to that.

MOORE: If she was a whore, you could have seen her naked without marrying her.

PYPER: What do you take me for? Do you think I have no respect? I married her to make an honest Protestant out of her.

MOORE: Of course, of course. Go on. What was she like?

PYPER: Unusual.

MOORE: How?

PYPER: You've heard the rumours?

MOORE: Every one. Wait, are you listening to this, Millen?

MILLEN: I'm coming over. Now, Crawford, have you got the hang of it?

CRAWFORD: I think so.

(MILLEN *thoroughly unmakes the bed*.)

MILLEN: Then make it yourself now, right?

(MILLEN *goes towards the others*.)

Go on. I've been listening.

MOORE: Right, Pyper.

PYPER: She started to take off her clothes very slowly, but very shyly. Well, I imagined it was very shy for a woman of her experience. When she was down to her petticoat, she stopped.

MOORE: Why?

29

PYPER: She asked me if I'd ever been alone with a woman like this before. A standard question for one of her profession, so I lied and said, yes, but never a Papist. When she heard this she told me I had a surprise coming. She took off her petticoat and there they were.

MOORE: What?

PYPER: Three legs.

MOORE: What?

PYPER: She had three legs. The middle one shorter than the normal two.

(CRAIG *starts to laugh*.)

MOORE: Don't laugh. That's the truth.

MILLEN: You believe that?

MOORE: I've heard that three-legged rumour before, but only in relation to nuns. There's this big convent in Portstewart –

PYPER: She could have started out as a nun. I don't know. I never got a chance to find out about her. She died on our wedding night.

MOORE: What happened?

PYPER: She bled to death.

MOORE: How?

PYPER: I sawed her middle leg off.

MOORE: Why?

PYPER: My duty as a Protestant.

MOORE: Where did you get a saw on your wedding night?

PYPER: I've heard the same rumour as you, Moore. In France I always carried a saw with me. It's overridden by nuns.

MOORE: Did you bury her after you murdered her?

PYPER: No. I ate her. Do you not remember I was starving in France?

MOORE: Pyper?

PYPER: What?

MOORE: I'm staying well clear of you.

MILLEN: That makes two of us. Come on, Willy.

(MOORE *and* MILLEN *go off*. CRAIG *remains*.)

CRAIG: You're some boy, Kenneth.

PYPER: Am I, David?

CRAIG: I've never met anybody like –

PYPER: Neither have I.

CRAIG: There'll be sport with you about.

PYPER: Will there be?

CRAIG: Go easy on Roulston a bit.

PYPER: Why?

CRAIG: He's nervous.

PYPER: David.

CRAIG: What?

PYPER: So am I. Have you a cigarette?

CRAIG: I thought you didn't smoke?

PYPER: I didn't. I do.

> (*They smoke in silence.* MILLEN *has been examining*
> *Crawford's bed.* MOORE *flicks through Roulston's Bible.*
> ROULSTON *watches him.*)

MILLEN: Do you call that making a bed?

CRAWFORD: I did my best.

MILLEN: Make it again.

CRAWFORD: Look, it's my bed. I've made it. I'll lie in it. Now
I've got my kit to get sorted out. Let me get on with it.

MILLEN: Then do it and make it snappy.

CRAWFORD: I'll do it in my own sweet time. You're not over
me.

MILLEN: Fighting back, Crawford?

CRAWFORD: I'm standing up for myself.

MILLEN: You're fighting back, man. You won't be much good
against the Kaiser if you've no gumption, will you? Get on
with it.

CRAIG: You didn't marry a French whore, did you?

PYPER: What makes you doubt it?

CRAIG: You don't strike me as a married man.

PYPER: Nor you me. Women in France are very beautiful. Like
women everywhere, as I'm sure a man of your experience
has found out.

CRAIG: I don't have much experience. Well, not that much.

PYPER: No, not that much. Like men everywhere.
Beautiful.

CRAIG: Men or women?

PYPER: What's the difference?

CRAIG: Why ask me? Do you expect me to know?

PYPER: I think you are a rare boy, David. When you want to be, as you say.

(PYPER *begins to put on the rest of his uniform.*)

CRAIG: Feeling a draught?

PYPER: I felt it a long time ago. I'm growing warmer.

CRAIG: What were you doing before enlisting?

PYPER: Whoring.

CRAIG: With three-legged French nuns?

PYPER: No. I was the whore.

ROULSTON: Do you often read the good book?

MOORE: This is yours, Roulston?

ROULSTON: Yes.

MOORE: Well thumbmarked.

ROULSTON: It should be. This Bible has been in my father's family for four generations.

MOORE: Four? Good work.

ROULSTON: Is there a particular book which interests you?

MOORE: No.

ROULSTON: I could recommend some of the psalms.

MOORE: Don't bother. I wasn't reading it. I was only looking for the dirty pictures.

(ROULSTON *snatches the Bible violently. He roars.*)

ROULSTON: Do you dare defile the word of God? Do you dare blaspheme against my Father?

(*After* ROULSTON'*s outburst there is sharp silence.* ROULSTON *sits on his bed, buries his head in his hands. The Bible falls to the floor.*)

MILLEN: You're going to burst your skull, son, before you give the Huns a chance to do it.

(CRAWFORD *goes and picks up Roulston's Bible.*)

CRAWFORD: Your Bible, Mr Roulston.

ROULSTON: Thank you.

CRAWFORD: It's all right.

ROULSTON: I don't know your name. I'm sorry.

CRAWFORD: Crawford, Martin Crawford, from Derry Town. And you?

ROULSTON: Roulston. Christopher Roulston.

CRAWFORD: No, I meant where are you from.

ROULSTON: Tyrone. Sion Mills. I was born there. Then the family moved.

CRAWFORD: I know it, Sion Mills. Good cricket club there.

ROULSTON: I never played, I'm afraid.

CRAWFORD: I haven't played much cricket. But I'm interested in games, all games. Boxing and football especially.

ROULSTON: Yes. Thank you.

CRAWFORD: I play for the town team every Saturday. Well, I played every Saturday. I don't know whether the army will let us play.

CRAIG: We'll get a game up here soon.

CRAWFORD: You play? What position?

CRAIG: Goals.

MILLEN: You've stolen my position, Craig.

MOORE: You're a rotten goalie.

MILLEN: I'm not that bad.

MOORE: You're pathetic. Anyway, Craig's the goalie.

CRAWFORD: Will we get permission to play a match?

MILLEN: If today's anything to go by.

MOORE: They must be easing us in.

CRAIG: We'll get a game.

(*A loud roar.* GEORGE ANDERSON *and* NAT MCILWAINE *enter, tossing their kit bags to each other.*)

ANDERSON: We're here, we're here. No cause for panic, ladies. The men are here.

MOORE: Belfast.

MILLEN: You'd never think it they're that quiet.

MCILWAINE: Line them up, line them up. We're ready for them.

ANDERSON: I spy a Taig. I spy a Taig.

MCILWAINE: Where? Tell me where?

ANDERSON: Use your nose, lad, use your nose. Have I not trained you to smell a Catholic within a mile of you? Get him.

(MCILWAINE *flings back his head, howls, rushes for* CRAWFORD.)

Tear his throat out.

(MCILWAINE *hurls* CRAWFORD *on to the bed, snarling and snapping.* ANDERSON *throws* MCILWAINE *off* CRAWFORD.)
Mad dog, mad dog, mad dog.
(ANDERSON *hurls* MCILWAINE *off the bed.*)

MILLEN: What the hell do yous two think you're doing?

ANDERSON: Defending this part of the realm –

MILLEN: Keep your defending for where it's needed across the water. Let that young lad go.

MCILWAINE: He's a Catholic bastard, he has no place in this regiment.

MILLEN: He's no Catholic. He's one of ours.

ANDERSON: Look at his eyes.

MOORE: Are you a Catholic, son?

CRAWFORD: No.

MILLEN: Let him go. Do you hear?

ANDERSON: I hear. I hear clearly.

(ANDERSON *lets* CRAWFORD *off the bed.* CRAWFORD *stands, then sits, turning his back on them all. He rises suddenly and exits. Soon afterwards* ROULSTON *follows him.*)

MC ILWAINE: He might deny he's a Catholic, but he wouldn't walk in our part of the shipyard.

MOORE: We might have known.

MCILWAINE: Known what?

MOORE: Shut up, you Belfast mouth.

MCILWAINE: Friendly company, eh Anderson?

ANDERSON: Warm as your mother's fireside, McIlwaine.

PYPER: Boys?

MCILWAINE: Look at this bucket.

ANDERSON: I know they're taking on all types, but are things that desperate?

PYPER: I'd like to show you something.

ANDERSON: I'd say you would if you'd one to show.

CRAIG: Leave it alone, Pyper.

PYPER: I want to be friendly. Watch this. Let me entertain you, boys.

(PYPER *rolls up his sleeve.*)

I observed to the company earlier how remarkably fine my skin is. They agreed. Do you?

ANDERSON: What kind of milksop –

PYPER: Now, I want to show you how someone with my remarkably fair skin can perform magic. A trick. A wee trick. Do you want to see it? Never mind. I'll show you. Here, look at my hands. Empty. Aren't they? Right. And nothing up my sleeve. Right. Feel my arms if you like. Feel them. Go on.

(ANDERSON *briefly feels* PYPER'S *arms.* MCILWAINE *tries to squeeze them into submission.* PYPER *hurls his effort aside.*)

Now that's cheating. None of that. Two bare arms. I clench each fist like this. Inside one of my hands something has appeared. I'll give it to whichever one of you guesses the correct hand. Come on, guess.

(*Silence.*)

Come on, guess. Guess. Guess.

(ANDERSON *touches* PYPER'S *right hand.* PYPER *punches him in the groin.* ANDERSON *screams.*)

MCILWAINE: You dirty bastard.

PYPER: That makes three of us. Warm as your mother's fireside, right, McIlwaine?

(MCILWAINE *helps* ANDERSON *on to a bed.*)

MCILWAINE: All right, Anderson, old boy? All right?

ANDERSON: Where is he?

MCILWAINE: Get your breath back. There'll be time to give him the hiding he's looking for. More than enough time. Get your breath back.

PYPER: Moore?

MOORE: What?

PYPER: Still going to stay clear of me?

MOORE: Clearer.

PYPER: What are you like in a fight, Moore?

MOORE: Clean, I fight clean. I fight straight.

PYPER: You're not going to survive.

MILLEN: We'll all survive. This is the best army on God's good earth.

PYPER: But we're the scum of it. We go first.

CRAIG: Not if we fight together.

PYPER: We will go first, David.

CRAIG: Pyper.

PYPER: We will go first, David.

(ROULSTON *and* CRAWFORD *enter.*)

MILLEN: Is that what you want, Pyper? Death? I've heard
about maniacs like you. The ones who sign up not to come
back. If that's what you've done, I'm warning you –

PYPER: I need some sense kicked into me, right?

MOORE: Right. More than right.

PYPER: Very much more than right. And I might get that kick
right here. I might survive from what I learn here. Right?
And who'll teach me? Other sons of Ulster, marching off to
war. A good war. A just war. Our war. The war of the elect
upon the damned, right? God's chosen will rise up and
fight. Will you rise up with me? The elect shall bond in
God's brotherhood. Right? Right. More than right. It's
good to be right. I'm sorry. I get carried away when I'm
right. I'm especially sorry for my violence against you,
Anderson. Will you accept my sorrow?

ANDERSON: McIlwaine, don't let that mad bastard anywhere
near me.

PYPER: I've studied anatomy. Perhaps I can ease your pain.

(PYPER *opens his penknife.*)

ANDERSON: Keep your hands away from me. I hate all doctors.

PYPER: Why are you afraid?

ANDERSON: I said keep away from me.

CRAIG: Kenneth, for God's sake.

PYPER: This is not the stuff we fashion heroes from.

ROULSTON: Pyper.

(PYPER *stands to attention and salutes.* CRAWFORD *enters.*)
If you are responsible for one more disturbance of the
peace in this barracks, I will be left with no option but to
report you.

PYPER: What, Roulston? What will you report? What have you
been doing, Christopher?

ROULSTON: Get out of the army now. Go to a doctor. You're
mad. He'll sign you out. Don't stay in this company. Get
out. Go.

PYPER: I will get out, Roulston, and do you know how? I'll die willingly. Will you? Yes. You can feel that. Death. You fear that. Death. And I know death. I'll let you know it. I'll take away your peace and that's the only disturbance I'm responsible for in this company. Right? Right. More than right.

(*Silence.*)

MILLEN: I've no time for this superstition.

MOORE: He'll learn the hard way. Are you all right, son?

CRAWFORD: As I'll ever be.

MILLEN: Good man.

(MILLEN *lies on his makeshift bed, as does* MOORE. ROULSTON *goes to his bed and begins to read the Bible.* CRAWFORD *goes over to read it with him.* MCILWAINE *looks after* ANDERSON. *Ignored by all except* CRAIG, PYPER *raises his left hand and with his penknife slits the front of it.* CRAIG *takes the shirt* PYPER *had given him. About to toss it at him,* CRAIG *hesitates, tears a sleeve from the shirt and attracts the others' attention by so doing. They watch as* CRAIG *bandages* PYPER's *bleeding hand.*)

CRAIG: Red hand.

PYPER: Red sky.

CRAIG: Ulster.

PYPER: Ulster.

PART 3: PAIRING

Ulster: Boa Island, Lough Erne, carvings [CRAIG *and* PYPER]; *a Protestant church* [ROULSTON *and* CRAWFORD]; *a suspended ropebridge* [MILLEN *and* MOORE]; *the Field, a lambeg drum* [MCILWAINE *and* ANDERSON].

The sound of water. Light up on Boa Island. CRAIG *rests, smoking.* PYPER *enters.*

CRAIG: Well?

PYPER: Good. Good place.

CRAIG: I hoped you'd like it.

PYPER: You rowed out here every day?

CRAIG: When I had the chance and I wanted to be on my island.

PYPER: Your island?

CRAIG: Sorry. Boa Island. I stand corrected. I meant when I wanted to be on my own.

PYPER: Nobody ever comes here?

CRAIG: Very few.

PYPER: Strange.

CRAIG: This place? Yes.

PYPER: The place is definitely strange, but strange too people shouldn't come.

CRAIG: Why should they come here?

PYPER: The carvings.

CRAIG: What are they?

PYPER: Signs.

CRAIG: Signs?

PYPER: Nothing. I'm talking rubbish.

CRAIG: Could you sculpt here again?

PYPER: What makes you ask that?

CRAIG: Just wondered.

PYPER: That's why you brought me here?

CRAIG: I just wanted to show it to you. That's all. I'm not putting any pressure on you.

(PYPER *laughs.*)

Why the laugh?

38

PYPER: Because I'm happy.

CRAIG: Good.

PYPER: Thanks.

CRAIG: What for?

(*Silence.*)

What for?

PYPER: You know.

CRAIG: No.

(*Silence.*)

PYPER: Saving my life. I want –

CRAIG: Kenneth, I don't want that brought up ever. Hear me? I only did what you would have done if it had been me. Not just me. Any of us. We need to forget.

PYPER: Do we?

CRAIG: Listen. I want to get away from the war. We're on leave. That long five months is behind us for a while. Leave passes quicker. I'm home now. I've brought you home. Home with me. I might never be able to do that again. When I walked into the Erne this morning, I just wanted to wash the muck of the world off myself. I thought it was on every part of me for life. But it's not. I'm clean again. I'm back. All right?

PYPER: You're going to shut me up?

CRAIG: Calm you down?

PYPER: Same difference.

CRAIG: I won't succeed.

PYPER: You might.

CRAIG: Tell me about the carvings. You're the smart boy. I always wanted to know about them.

PYPER: What?

CRAIG: I don't know. Tell me.

(*Lights fade on Boa Island.*)

Lights up on the church. ROULSTON *kneels.*

CRAWFORD: I think we should leave this church.

ROULSTON: I can't leave this church.

CRAWFORD: It's not helping you in here.

ROULSTON: I'm not asking for help. I'm asking for strength.

CRAWFORD: You proved your strength beside me.

ROULSTON: No.

CRAWFORD: Why ask for more?

ROULSTON: No, no. I have to.

CRAWFORD: Are you afraid to go back?

ROULSTON: Have I left the front?

CRAWFORD: You're strong already, man. Now prove it. Leave this church with me.

ROULSTON: I can't.

CRAWFORD: Why not?

ROULSTON: Because – because I have to give thanks. That we're alive. All of us. Does that not strike you as God's will?

CRAWFORD: Why God's will?

ROULSTON: The day we joined up, all eight of us, still living. How many other days were as blessed? How many other days were as lucky?

Roulstons belief

CRAWFORD: So you admit there was luck in it?

ROULSTON: There's more to it than that.

CRAWFORD: Such as what? Such as?

ROULSTON: Why do you always question?

CRAWFORD: Because you never do.

ROULSTON: That's not true. I never stop asking myself questions. Why do you think I'm not still a clergyman?

CRAWFORD: Because you don't believe.

ROULSTON: What?

CRAWFORD: You don't believe. *⇒ Belief challenge*

ROULSTON: I believe too much.

CRAWFORD: You don't believe in Christ. You don't believe in God. You don't believe in yourself. If you do, prove it. (*Silence.*)

ROULSTON: How?

CRAWFORD: Leave.

ROULSTON: I can't.

CRAWFORD: You see, you don't believe. (*Lights fade on the church.*)

40

Lights up on the bridge. MILLEN *and* MOORE *stand on one end.*

MOORE: I can't cross it, Johnny, I can't. I want to but I'm not able.

MILLEN: You have to try.

MOORE: Tomorrow.

MILLEN: No, you have to do it now.

MOORE: I'll fall.

MILLEN: You won't.

MOORE: Why have we been spared?

MILLEN: Spared what?

MOORE: Johnny, I can't go back.

MILLEN: You've told me that already.

MOORE: I wouldn't tell anyone else.

MILLEN: Get to your feet and start walking to the bloody rock and back.

MOORE: I'm getting sick just looking down.

MILLEN: Don't look anywhere but straight in front of you.

MOORE: You do it first.

MILLEN: It'll make no difference. Walk.

MOORE: No.

MILLEN: We're not leaving till you cross it.

MOORE: I'm tired. I'm frightened. I don't want to go on. I can't.

MILLEN: Come on.

MOORE: All the dead.

MILLEN: You've said we've been spared. You won't fall.

MOORE: I'll die first.

MILLEN: No.

MOORE: Why did you bring me here?

MILLEN: Walk.

MOORE: I can't.

MILLEN: Then stay where you are.

MOORE: I keep hearing the dead.

MILLEN: It's only the water beneath you. You've heard it before.

MOORE: It's guns.

MILLEN: The guns are over there. You're home.

41

MOORE: The guns are home.

MILLEN: Stand up, come on, stand up.

MOORE: I've lost my nerve, you bastard. Do you not see I've lost my nerve? I can't move. Leave me alone. I want to fall here. I want to die.

(MILLEN *shakes* MOORE.)

MILLEN: You've lost your nerve, have you? Get over there and get it back. Get over there and come back in one piece.

(MOORE *is now standing on the bridge.*)

MOORE: I won't make it.

MILLEN: You will. I'm with you.

MOORE: Where's the rest of them?

MILLEN: They're with you. They want you to cross.

MOORE: Pyper, Roulston, Craig.

MILLEN: I said they're with you.

MOORE: Anderson, Crawford.

MILLEN: They're all here.

MOORE: McIlwaine.

MILLEN: Every one of them.

MOORE: Millen.

MILLEN: I'm behind you. I'm here.

MOORE: Johnny.

MILLEN: I'm here. I'm listening. You've missed one out.

MOORE: Who?

MILLEN: Think.

MOORE: Who?

MILLEN: He's a weaver. A Coleraine man. Half-blind. So he won't see much if he looks up or down. Do you remember him? He saw a horse being shot. His heart went out to the horse. Now he's seen men being shot. He came back. His heart hasn't come back. It was cut out of him. His heart's over there. Do you know who he is?

MOORE: Yes.

MILLEN: Walk over to him.

MOORE: Are you with me still?

MILLEN: No. You're by yourself.

(MOORE *takes another step on to the bridge. Lights fade on the bridge.*)

42

Lights up on the field. MCILWAINE *and* ANDERSON *sprawl on the ground. Beside them a lambeg drum.*

MCILWAINE: Good day.

ANDERSON: Beautiful.

MCILWAINE: How was she sounding?

ANDERSON: Perfect.

MCILWAINE: Great drum.

ANDERSON: The best.

MCILWAINE: See this, this is holy ground.

ANDERSON: The Field?

MCILWAINE: The Field. Holiest spot in Ulster. I'm glad we come here, laughed at or not.

ANDERSON: Who was laughing at us?

MCILWAINE: They all were.

ANDERSON: I didn't hear them laughing. If I had, I'd have knocked their teeth in. When did you see them laughing?

MCILWAINE: Everyone. Every single one. .

ANDERSON: Who?

MCILWAINE: Willy Moore for one. And his pal, Millen. I asked them to march with us. And they refused. And why? Because it wasn't the Twelfth of July. Look, said I. We weren't here on the Twelfth of July. We were over across. We couldn't march. Now we're back. We can march in battalion. I'll carry the drum. Yous carry the banner. Romp up a bit of support. We'll make a fair show of Orangemen. We'll march to the Field. The bastard laughed at me.

ANDERSON: Moore?

MCILWAINE: When was the last time you heard Moore laugh?

ANDERSON: How should I know? Anyway, I didn't hear them laughing.

MCILWAINE: Then why would they not join us?

ANDERSON: They'd marched on the Twelfth.

MCILWAINE: Why shouldn't they march again? Why shouldn't they march with us? We're the returning heroes. We should be marched with. We are the boys. We should be celebrated. Shouldn't we? I'm asking shouldn't we? Are you going to answer me?

ANDERSON: Hold your tongue. You've had enough I see.

43

MCILWAINE: I haven't started. And don't preach to me.

ANDERSON: You want more?

MCILWAINE: If I can find it.

ANDERSON: Look beside you. It's there.

(MCILWAINE *finds the bottle of Bushmills, opens it, is about to take a slug from it, roars with laughter, leaves down the bottle, cups his hands into fists.*)

MCILWAINE: Georgie?

ANDERSON: What do you want? I know you're up to some badness when you use my Christian name. I'm warning you.

MCILWAINE: No badness. Just a trick. Remember this?

ANDERSON: Remember this? Remember what?

MCILWAINE: I have remarkably fine skin for a man. The others agree. Do you?

ANDERSON: What's got into you?

MCILWAINE: I'll close my empty hands. If you guess which one there's something –

ANDERSON: Cut that out.

MCILWAINE: You'll get it –

ANDERSON: I said cut it out.

MCILWAINE: You walked into that one, boy.

ANDERSON: You mightn't walk out of it.

MCILWAINE: He's some fighter though. Pyper. Who would have thought it?

ANDERSON: Who indeed?

MCILWAINE: You said he was a milksop.

ANDERSON: There's still something rotten there. That time Craig threw himself on him to save him.

MCILWAINE: What about them?

ANDERSON: The look on their faces. Something rotten.

MCILWAINE: What?

ANDERSON: Who gives a Fenian's curse? Show us that bottle.

MCILWAINE: Hold your horses. Here. Pour us a drop in here.

(ANDERSON *pours whiskey into* MCILWAINE's *cupped hands. He opens his hands and whiskey pours on to the ground.*)

Something rotten.

ANDERSON: What the hell are you doing? Waste of good whiskey.

MCILWAINE: It's no good. It's no good.

ANDERSON: The whiskey?

MCILWAINE: Everything. It's no good here on your own. No good without the speakers. No good without the bands, no good without the banners. Without the chaps. No good on your own. Why did we come here to be jeered at? Why did we come here, Anderson?

ANDERSON: To beat a drum.

(*Lights fade on the Field.*)

Lights up on Boa. PYPER *studies the stone carving. Lights up on the church.* ROULSTON *stands.*

CRAIG: Well, what are they?

PYPER: Don't rush me.

CRAIG: You've had enough time.

PYPER: I don't think these have anything to do with time.

ROULSTON: When I came through this battle, do you know what I felt?

CRAWFORD: Blessed?

ROULSTON: More than that.

CRAWFORD: What?

ROULSTON: Chosen.

CRAIG: They don't look like men or women.

PYPER: Depends on the man or woman.

CRAIG: They could be either.

PYPER: They could be both.

ROULSTON: Saved.

CRAWFORD: To survive?

ROULSTON: Something else.

CRAWFORD: What?

CRAIG: What do you think they are?

PYPER: Men and women? Men and women are gods.

CRAWFORD: I asked what.

ROULSTON: I realized for the first time what it means to be of the elect.

CRAIG: What kind of gods?

PYPER: Domestic gods. Ancestral gods. Industrial gods. Living gods. You know them. You live with them. You fight with them.

45

CRAIG: And which am I?

PYPER: Living.

CRAIG: How?

CRAWFORD: What does it mean, being of the elect?

ROULSTON: That you're the Son of God.

PYPER: This is how.

(PYPER *takes* CRAIG'*s hands and touches the carvings with them*.)

Touch. You have their touch on you. Touch. Live.

CRAIG: That's not what I was asking.

CRAWFORD: Explain what you're saying exactly.

PYPER: It's the only way I can answer you.

ROULSTON: Son of God, Son of Man – I can't preach any more.

CRAIG: That's no answer. I want something more from you. I want to understand this place. To understand you. Explain yourself to me here.

CRAWFORD: I don't want your preaching.

PYPER: I could only explain myself when I could see, not just with my eyes, but with my hands. They've stopped?

CRAIG: See. See now. See what's in front of you.

PYPER: How?

CRAIG: Start again. With your eyes. Carve. Carve me.

ROULSTON: It's beyond language.

CRAWFORD: Why did you bring me here?

ROULSTON: I grew up in this church.

CRAWFORD: You grew stunted in it. Didn't you? Well, didn't you?

PYPER: You're on this island.

CRAIG: Who's with me?

PYPER: I am. Flesh. Stone. David. Goliath. Why did David save Goliath's life? For Goliath diminished into nothing through David's faith and sacrifice. Was David cruel to save Goliath from death? Because Goliath in his brutality, in his ugliness, wanted death. David would not let him die. He wanted to rescue Goliath from becoming a god. A dead god.

ROULSTON: There was once a boy. This boy spent so long in church they said he was born there. The boy only wanted

to please his fathers, earthly and heavenly. But neither
father believed, by word nor passion, in him, the boy. The
father's lack of belief stunted the boy. He could not grow in
his faith. Without faith how could the boy grow into a
man? For the only men he knew were men of firm faith.
Faith in themselves. In their world. In their own heavenly
father. The boy tried to assert his faith in their world by
serving the church of his heavenly father. He failed. He
turned instead to serve the army of the king, his God's
anointed. He served. He lived. He lives. Now he realizes –
he recognizes –

(PYPER *points to the carving.*)

PYPER: Did you see the stone, David?

ROULSTON: Yes.

PYPER: Do you hear what he's saying?

ROULSTON: Yes.

PYPER: You're speaking to a stone. And this stone destroys
whoever touches it.

ROULSTON: Do you not see who I am? I am Christ. Son of
Man. Son of God.

(*He continues softly and simultaneously with* PYPER'*s speech.*)
In the beginning is the Word. And the Word is within me.
And the Word is without me. For I am the Word and the
Word is mine.

(CRAWFORD *turns his back on* ROULSTON.)

PYPER: I turn people into stone. Women and men. Into gods. I
turned my ancestors into Protestant gods, so I could rebel
against them. I would not serve. I turned my face from
their thick darkness. But the same gods have brought me
back. Alive through you. They wanted their outcast. I have
returned with you to worship Enniskillen and the Boyne.
My life has been saved for their lives, their deaths. I
thought I'd left the gods behind. But maybe they sent me
away, knowing what would happen. I went to Paris. I
carved. I carved out something rotten, something
evil.

CRAIG: What evil, Kenneth?

CRAWFORD: Who cares?

CRAIG: Tell me.

(Lights fade on Boa Island.)

CRAWFORD: Who cares what you think you are? I don't give a damn. What kind of boy do you think I am? You seem to think I'm soft in the head. Just like Anderson and McIlwaine did on the first day to me, you're doing now. Trying to knock the living daylights out of my mind and senses – through ganging up. They ganged up with each other. You gang up with Christ. Well, listen, keep him to yourself. I'm not interested in either of you. Christ never did much for me, and I don't think he's done much for you. What did he give me? Look at it. What am I? I'll tell you. I'm a soldier that risks his neck for no cause other than the men he's fighting with. I've seen enough to see through empires and kings and countries. I know the only side worth supporting is your own sweet self. I'll support you because if it comes to the crunch I hope you'll support me. That's all I know. That's all I feel. I don't believe in Christ. I believe in myself. I believe in you only in so far as you're a soldier like myself. No more, no less. That's what I have to say about your outburst. It was a disgrace. Do you have anything to say to defend yourself?

(Lights fade on the church.)

Lights up on the bridge. MOORE *has commenced his crossing. Lights up on the field.*

MOORE: No more.

MILLEN: You have to move one way or the other.

MOORE: I can't see where I'm going.

MILLEN: Keep going. Don't look down. Don't listen. Just get to where you're heading.

(MCILWAINE beats the lambeg drum with his fist.)

MOORE: I'm back there again.

MILLEN: You're here with me now.

MOORE: You were there, I didn't want to leave it alive.

MILLEN: I said don't think of anything. Just move.

MOORE: No.

MILLEN: Move.

48

MOORE: I'm going to die. They're com'ng at me from all sides.
    (MCILWAINE *beats louder on the lambeg.*)
ANDERSON: Are you going to play it?
MCILWAINE: What for?
MOORE: Keep them away from me.
ANDERSON: Celebrate.
MCILWAINE: What?
MILLEN: Keep them away from yourself.
ANDERSON: Us.
MOORE: I can't keep on much longer.
    (MCILWAINE *kicks the lambeg.*)
ANDERSON: Why did you do that?
MCILWAINE: Get it out of my sight.
ANDERSON: It's only a drum.
MILLEN: Close your eyes.
MCILWAINE: Know what I'm thinking about?
MILLEN: Keep taking your breath.
MCILWAINE: That boat.
MOORE: I see nothing before me.
ANDERSON: The *Titanic*?
MILLEN: The end's in sight.
ANDERSON: What brings the *Titanic* into your mind?
MCILWAINE: The drum. The noise of it. It's like the sound she
    made hitting the Lagan.
ANDERSON: We weren't to blame. No matter what they say.
MCILWAINE: Papists?
    (MCILWAINE *spits.*)
MOORE: I'm drenched.
MILLEN: That's with sweat.
MOORE: Not with muck? Not with flesh? Not with blood?
MILLEN: Just with sweat.
MOORE: I think it's blood. But it's not my own. I never saw
    that much blood, Johnny.
MILLEN: It's not ours.
MOORE: The whole world is bleeding. Nobody can stop it.
    (MOORE *slowly continues his crossing.*)
ANDERSON: Every nail they hammered into the *Titanic*, they
    cursed the Pope. That's what they say.

MCILWAINE: There was a lot of nails in the *Titanic*.

ANDERSON: And he still wasn't cursed enough.

MCILWAINE: Every nail we hammered into the *Titanic*, we'll die in the same amount in this cursed war. That's what I say.

ANDERSON: What are you talking about?

MCILWAINE: The war's cursed. It's good for nothing. A waste of time. We won't survive. We're all going to die for nothing. Pyper was right. I know now. We're on the *Titanic*. We're all going down. Women and children first. Women and children. Damn the Pope. Let me die damning him.

ANDERSON: Catch yourself on. You're not dying. None of us are dying. Here.

(MCILWAINE *grabs the whiskey bottle, slumps back.*)

MOORE: Are you a soldier, Millen? Are you a good soldier? Am I? I think there's no such thing any more. There are only cowards, and the worst learn to hide it best. I can't hide it any more. I won't be back. Let me go. Let me fall.

MILLEN: Here, take my hand. Take my hand.

(MILLEN *holds out his hand. Beyond its reach,* MOORE *raises his hand. They do not meet.*)

Have you got hold of it?

MOORE: I don't know.

MILLEN: Just feel it. Feel around it.

(MOORE's *hand feels the air.*)

Can you touch the fingers? Can you get the feel of the palm? Do you find its strength? Come on, Willy, can you find it?

MOORE: Yes.

MILLEN: Right, that hand's holding you up. You won't fall if you move. Do you believe that?

MOORE: Yes.

MILLEN: Walk to the other side. There's people waiting for you over there. Who are they?

MOORE: All the dead people.

MILLEN: No. All the living. Do you see them? Who are they?

MOORE: I don't recognize them.

MILLEN: You do. Name them. One by one. Who are they?
  (*Lights fade on the bridge.*)

ANDERSON: Are you all right now? I said it before, and I mean
  it this time, you've had enough, boy. I want to hear no
  more chat like this.

MCILWAINE: Give my head peace.

ANDERSON: You're raving drunk.

MCILWAINE: Just raving.

ANDERSON: We should be getting back soon.

MCILWAINE: I can't leave here. Not yet anyway.

ANDERSON: Do you want to pitch camp here for the night? If
  you do, you're on your own.

MCILWAINE: I'm always on my own. Always have been.

ANDERSON: Because you're a hateful git.

MCILWAINE: It was a sign of what we're in for. What we've let
  ourselves in for.

ANDERSON: The bloody *Titanic* went down because it hit an
  iceberg.

MCILWAINE: The pride of Belfast went with it.

ANDERSON: You're not going to meet many icebergs on the
  front, are you? So what are you talking about?

MCILWAINE: The war is our punishment.

ANDERSON: There's more than Belfast in this war.

MCILWAINE: But Belfast will be lost in this war. The whole of
  Ulster will be lost. We're not making a sacrifice. Jesus,
  you've seen this war. We are the sacrifice. What's keeping
  us over there? We're all going mad. Some of us, like Pyper,
  were mad before going. Others are getting that way, look at
  Moore. He won't be back. He'll be in a home for the rest of
  his life. Where I'll be too. Crawford's turning into a
  machine and I'm going lunatic –

ANDERSON: I'm listening to no more of this drunken rambling.

MCILWAINE: It is not drunken rambling. You're listening to no
  more of what I have to say because you've already said it
  yourself. You already know what's happened to yourself,
  but you won't admit it, will you? You can't admit it, and I
  can. *I can.* Oh, for Christ's sake, Georgie, stop me talking

like this. Drown me out, will you? Stop me. Give me noise. Give me the docks. Give me the yard. Steel banging against steel. Hammer in my hands. Fill me with noise, man. Stop me hearing myself. Stop me.

(ANDERSON *grabs* MCILWAINE'S *fists, brings them down heavily and repeatedly on the lambeg, until* MCILWAINE *shakes him off and falls heavily against the drum.*)

Lights up on all areas. There is stillness. MCILWAINE *rises from the drum.*

ANDERSON: All right?

MCILWAINE: (*Looks at his hands.*) They're not bleeding. To play this brute of a drum your flesh must bleed. Mine isn't. I'm doing it wrong and I'm going to do it right this year above all others. Help me into this.

(MCILWAINE *grabs the lambeg by its straps.*)

ANDERSON: For God's sake, man, it's late.

MCILWAINE: Help me into this, I'm telling you.

(ANDERSON *helps* MCILWAINE *into the drum.*)

ANDERSON: Will you go after this?

MCILWAINE: We'll see.

ANDERSON: Will you at least sleep it off?

MCILWAINE: When was the last time I slept?

ANDERSON: How do I know?

MCILWAINE: When was the last time you slept?

ANDERSON: I sleep sound.

MCILWAINE: I think I've been asleep for years. I want the sound of this boy to rouse me. If it doesn't, I can't go back there.

ANDERSON: You'll go back to the front, if I've to carry you. You won't disgrace yourself or your breed or where you work. Now get it over with, will you?

MCILWAINE: You've to do your bit as well.

ANDERSON: How?

MCILWAINE: Speak. Speak loud and clear. Let them hear you in Belfast. Let the Fenians hear it everywhere. Let the Hun hear the sons of Ulster preaching war.

ANDERSON: You are off your head.

MCILWAINE: Speak, do you hear me? Roar it out, Anderson.

(MCILWAINE *hammers on the drum. Light fades on the field.*)

ROULSTON: I'm cold. We'll leave.

CRAWFORD: We'll stay.

ROULSTON: Why?

CRAWFORD: Do you not want me to say my prayers? Wait there. Wait until I'm ready.

(CRAWFORD *kneels. Light fades on the church.*)

CRAIG: Why have you told me about her? Why have you told me about her?

PYPER: To let you know what you saved.

(CRAIG *rises.*)

Perhaps I misjudged.

(*Light fades on the island.*)

MOORE: Craig?

MILLEN: Craig's there, yes. Do you know him?

MOORE: Courage of a lion. Blacksmith. Risked his life for Pyper's. Together for eternity now. Good man, Craig. Two of them. Good men. Did Pyper come back from the dead that time he fell? I saw it. I saw Craig, what he did. He blew his own breath into Pyper's mouth. It was a kiss.

MILLEN: Who else is there? Is Roulston there?

MOORE: I think he is, but I can't fathom him. I don't think he's a holy man, but he tries to be. Crawford keeps his feet on the ground. They make a funny pair. Not like you and me. Not like Anderson and McIlwaine. Anderson is turning his back on me. McIlwaine is still looking.

MILLEN: Walk to them.

(MOORE *continues his crossing.*)

MOORE: I've seen you all my life, Millen. You could always lead me where you wanted. I was afraid of not doing as you bid. Who leads you?

MILLEN: Top brass. I do as I'm told. I make no complaints. If they order me to put my hand in the fire, for the sake of what I believe in, what they believe in, I'd do it willingly. You have to do that as well, Moore. That's the only way you'll come back alive. Keep crossing. Keep working at it.

MOORE: This bridge is a piece of cloth. It needs colouring. I'm a dyer. When I step across it, my two feet are my eyes. They put a shape on it. They give it a colour. And the colour is my life and all I've done with it. Not much, but it's mine. So I'll keep going to its end.

MILLEN: Once you've done that, nothing can stop you coming back.

MOORE: Except top brass.

MILLEN: How?

MOORE: If they order me to fall?

MILLEN: You fall.

(MOORE *has arrived at the bridge's end.*)

MOORE: Millen? When I touched your hand, I smelt bread of it. I smelt life.

MILLEN: Mine or yours?

MOORE: The two. Two lives. We're going to lose them. We're going to die.

(*Silence.*)

MILLEN: No.

MOORE: Die together as we lived together. I can see death as sure as I can touch your hand. Your hand's cold, but death will warm it. It's like an oven. It's roasting. It's waiting for all of us. You're turning white. You're like ice. But you'll melt in the oven. You'll bake there. You'll lose your smell of bread, and you'll find the smell of death. You'll burn.

MILLEN: Stop this. Come back here, Moore, to me. Do you hear me? Come back over to me. Come back from the dead.

(*Lights fade on the bridge. Light on the church.*)

CRAWFORD: Christopher?

ROULSTON: Yes.

CRAWFORD: Do you hear confession?

ROULSTON: Confession?

CRAWFORD: A Papist sacrament. You tell your sins and secrets. To a priest. I want you to hear mine. Remember when Anderson smelt a Catholic? He half did. My mother's Fenian. She never converted. I'm sure I was baptized one sometime. No one else knows that. Can you keep a secret?

ROULSTON: I don't believe your secret.

CRAWFORD: I'll break your mouth if you tell it.

54

ROULSTON: This is not funny, Martin.

CRAWFORD: I challenge you to keep your mouth shut.

ROULSTON: Challenge?

CRAWFORD: Come on, I'll fight you for it.

ROULSTON: Where do you think you're standing? A public house? This is a church.

CRAWFORD: Who gives a damn? It's not my church.

ROULSTON: It's mine.

CRAWFORD: Come on then, Proddy. I'll fight you for it. Come on, planter. Winner takes all.

(ROULSTON *turns to leave.* CRAWFORD *grabs him in a stranglehold.*)

Do you submit? Or do you resist?

(ROULSTON *hurls* CRAWFORD *aside.*)

ROULSTON: I'm warning you.

CRAWFORD: I'll do the warning.

(CRAWFORD *trips* ROULSTON, *rapidly breaking his fall, spreadeagling him.*)

Fight back. Can you?

ROULSTON: Please stop.

CRAWFORD: No, fight. Fight me.

(ROULSTON *lashes out at* CRAWFORD. *It is no use.*)

ROULSTON: Let me up. if anyone enters this church –

CRAWFORD: Tell them I'm a Fenian. They'll join in.

(CRAWFORD *slaps* ROULSTON *violently about the face.*)

Come on, Christ, turn the other cheek.

(ROULSTON *spits into* CRAWFORD'*s face.*)

As good a beginning as any.

(CRAWFORD *releases* ROULSTON. ROULSTON *rises slowly. Suddenly he attacks* CRAWFORD, *who makes only a feeble attempt at defence.*)

ROULSTON: Don't ever attempt to humiliate me again. Do you hear? I said, do you hear?

CRAWFORD: Yes, Pyper. Yes, Anderson. Yes, McIlwaine. Yes, lout. They're all one, aren't they? And now you're one with them. You're one with us. Blasphemer, brawling in the church. No better, no worse. Sorry about that. You had it coming. One or the other would have given you the same

lesson someday. Weren't you lucky it was me? Weren't you lucky it was here? Now you can march out of it with me, a soldier, a man, a brute beast. You're not Christ. You're a man. One man among many. (*Pause.*) Want to join me someday in a game of football? I've got you boxing.
(*Lights fade on church. Light rises on the island.*)

CRAIG: Why did you kill her?

PYPER: I had to. And she killed herself.

CRAIG: You drove her there. You drove her to do it, if all you say is true. Is this another test? Another riddle? See if I can answer a shocking one? Well, I can't. You've got me. So tell me straight why you killed her.

PYPER: She killed herself. She killed herself. She killed herself. Because she was stupid enough to believe that I was all she had to live for. Me. What would I have brought her? The same end, but a lot later, and not with the dignity of doing it with her own hand. I'm one of the gods, I bring destruction. Remember?

CRAIG: Don't try that smart talk to get yourself out of this.

PYPER: What more's to be said? She took her life. She did something with it, finally and forever. I thought I was doing the same when I cleared out of this country and went to do something with my heart and my eyes and my hands and my brains. Something I could not do here as the eldest son of a respectable family whose greatest boast is that in their house Sir Edward Carson, saviour of their tribe, danced in the finest gathering Armagh had ever seen. I escaped Carson's dance. While you were running with your precious motors to bring in his guns, I escaped Carson's dance, David. I got out to create, not destroy. But the gods wouldn't allow that. I could not create. That's the real horror of what I found in Paris, not the corpse of a dead whore. I couldn't look at my life's work, for when I saw my hands working they were not mine but the hands of my ancestors, interfering, and I could not be rid of that interference. I could not create. I could only preserve. Preserve my flesh and blood, what I'd seen, what I'd learned. It wasn't enough. I was contaminated. I smashed

56

my sculpture and I rejected any woman who would
continue my breed. I destroyed one to make that certain.
And I would destroy my own life. I would take up arms at
the call of my Protestant fathers. I would kill in their name
and I would die in their name. To win their respect would
be my sole act of revenge, revenge for the bad joke they had
played on me in making me sufficiently different to believe
I was unique, when my true uniqueness lay only in how
alike them I really was. And then the unseen obstacle in my
fate. I met you.

CRAIG: What do you want from me?

PYPER: What you want.

(*Silence.*)

CRAIG: You said you wanted to die. I know what you mean. I
didn't want to die, but I know what you mean. I wanted
war. I wanted a fight. I felt I was born for it, and it alone. I
felt that because I wanted to save somebody else in war, but
that somebody else was myself. I wanted to change what I
am. Instead I saved you, because of what I am. I want you
to live, and I know some one of us is going to die. I think
it's me. Sometimes I look at myself and I see a horse. There
are hounds about me, and I'm following them to death. I'm
a dying breed, boy. I can't talk in your riddles. I used to
worry even up till today, when you talked to me like that,
in case you were setting me up. I don't worry any more. It
was yourself you were talking to. But when you talk to me,
you see me. Eyes, hands. Not carving. Just seeing. And I
didn't save you that day. I saw you. And from what I saw I
knew I'm not like you. I am you.

PYPER: David.

CRAIG: What?

PYPER: Name. Say it. Want to.

PYPER: More riddles?

PYPER: No. Talk straight from now on.

CRAIG: Why?

PYPER: Quicker.

CRAIG: Dance.

PYPER: The gods are watching.

CRAIG: The gods.

PYPER: Protestant gods.

CRAIG: Carson.

PYPER: King.

CRAIG: Ulster.

PYPER: Ulster.

CRAIG: Stone.

PYPER: Flesh.

CRAIG: Carson is asking you to dance in the temple of the Lord.

PYPER: Dance.

(*Lights fade on the island. Lights on the field. Then*
ANDERSON *helps* MCILWAINE *out of the drum*.)

ANDERSON: Content?

MCILWAINE: Content. Very content. Look.

(MCILWAINE *shows* ANDERSON *his hands*.)

ANDERSON: Remarkably fine skin.

MCILWAINE: Aye, for a man.

(*They laugh*.)

ANDERSON: Wash it off.

MCILWAINE: No way. Never. I can go back now. Georgie?

ANDERSON: Enough's enough.

MCILWAINE: Did I play well?

ANDERSON: They would have heard you for miles. You've
wakened the dead.

MCILWAINE: I wanted to. I'm a good soldier?

ANDERSON: The best.

MCILWAINE: A good worker?

ANDERSON: None better.

MCILWAINE: I want to stay the night here.

ANDERSON: Come on, man, come on.

MCILWAINE: You didn't do your bit. You didn't speak.

ANDERSON: I listened.

MCILWAINE: That's not good enough. You're the Grand
Master. I have just appointed my friend, Mr George
Anderson, to the position of Grand Master of the Orange
Lodges of Ireland. I demand silence. He will speak as is his
duty.

ANDERSON: Some other day.

MCILWAINE: No, I want a speech.

ANDERSON: Come on now.

MCILWAINE: I said I want a good speech. Speak.

ANDERSON: What do you want me to say?

MCILWAINE: What I want to hear.

ANDERSON: Brethren of the true faith, fellow Orangemen,
comrades-in-arms, the sons of Ulster today give their
service and in many cases their lives to the good fight of
king and country in many parts of the world. Just as they
have often given them before. But we do not lose sight of
the battle that rages for our lands, our people, our spirit,
our souls in this country where we belong. I do not speak of
the Hun, dire enemy though he may be, when I speak of
the enemy now. I speak of the Fenian. The Catholic traitor
that will corrupt our young, deflower our womenfolk and
destroy all that we hold most dear. Our beloved religion.

MCILWAINE: Where we fought for our glorious religion on the
green, grassy slopes of the Boyne.

ANDERSON: The Boyne is not a river of water. It is a river of
blood. The blood that flows through our veins, brothers.
And this blood will not be drained into the sewers of an
Irish republic. We will not recognize this republic. We will
fight this republic. We will fight it as we have fought in
other centuries to answer our king's call. To answer God's
call. We will draw our men from the farms, from the
townlands and commerce of our province, our beloved
Ulster. And our men will follow that call to freedom. They
will fight for it. They will kill for it. They will die for it.
They will die for it. Die, die, die.

(ANDERSON *starts to fall.* MCILWAINE *holds him up.*)

MCILWAINE: Go on.

ANDERSON: No, no more. I've done my bit.

MCILWAINE: Are you sinking?

ANDERSON: Pyper the bastard was right. It's all lies. We're
going to die. It's all lies. We're going to die for nothing.
Let me go. It's all lies.

MCILWAINE: All right, now, all right.

ANDERSON: We'll never be back here.

MCILWAINE: We'll never leave here.
ANDERSON: We have to go back.
MCILWAINE: Can you manage walking?
ANDERSON: No. Let me rest. Let me rest.
MCILWAINE: Right. Right you be.

Lights up on the bridge. MOORE *and* MILLEN *are on opposing sides still.*
MOORE: You'll never lead me again. I'm on my own here, you're on your own there. That's the way it should be.
MILLEN: Who put you there?
MOORE: You did, I did, they did.
MILLEN: Top brass?
MOORE: No such thing. Top brass are supposed to give orders. You follow orders. I follow orders. But orders are only orders when you follow them.
MILLEN: If you've stopped following orders, stay where you are.
MOORE: I haven't stopped following orders. I've started giving them.
MILLEN: You want me to leave?
MOORE: No. (*Pause.*) Wait for me.
MILLEN: Why should I? You seem to think I know nothing.
MOORE: You know enough.
MILLEN: I don't know you.
MOORE: Who led me? Who saved me?
MILLEN: Who?
MOORE: Thanks.

Lights up on all areas.
PYPER: Well?
CRAIG: Water.
PYPER: You're a rare buckcat, Craig. Rare.
CRAIG: I'm a hound, pup. No buckcat.
PYPER: Whatever you say, sir.
ANDERSON: We'll never make it home tonight.
MCILWAINE: Then we'll stay.
ROULSTON: Did I hurt you?

60

CRAWFORD: Yes.
ROULSTON: Good.
CRAWFORD: Good.
PYPER: Are you ready then?
CRAIG: As I'll ever be.
ANDERSON: This is the place for us.
MCILWAINE: Just perch ourselves where we are.
MILLEN: Move.
PYPER: Coming with me?
CRAWFORD: Come on.
MCILWAINE: Can you not sleep?
CRAIG: To the front.
ANDERSON: I can't sleep, Nat. No sleep.
ROULSTON: Out we go.
MILLEN: Move.
MOORE: March.

(*The drum resounds.*)

PART 4: BONDING

A trench, the Somme. MCILWAINE, *the* YOUNGER PYPER *and* MILLEN *are awake. The others sleep.*

MCILWAINE: You'd think they were dead, it's that quiet.

PYPER: Yes.

MILLEN: When do you think word'll come?

PYPER: When we're ready.

MILLEN: What have we to do with it?

PYPER: We do the attacking.

MILLEN: We don't do the ordering.

PYPER: You above all are not beginning to panic, Millen?

MILLEN: I've been panicking since the last leave, Pyper.

MCILWAINE: There won't be much of daylight before we're going over.

MILLEN: I think this is it. I think this is going to be the end.

PYPER: Millen, for Christ's sake.

MILLEN: I can't help it. I know this time.

MCILWAINE: Nobody knows nothing here.

PYPER: Any officers about?

MCILWAINE: One passed twenty minutes ago. Told us to get some rest.

MILLEN: I saw him. Useless bugger. Surely to God they're not going to trust us with that piece of work. Where do they dig them out of anyway? Superior rank, is that it? Superior, my arse.

MCILWAINE: Keep talking like that and it'll be a court martial you'll be facing, not –

MILLEN: Let me face it and I'll tell them straight.

PYPER: Tell them what?

MILLEN: What they're doing to us.

MCILWAINE: And that will stop them? That'll stop us? Save your breath for running. It's a bit late to start crying now.

MILLEN: I'm not crying.

MCILWAINE: You're damn near it. Pyper? You come from a swanky family, don't you?

PYPER: Why ask that now?

MCILWAINE: I'm just beginning to wonder what you're doing down with us instead of being with them.

PYPER: And who are they?

MCILWAINE: Top brass.

PYPER: I'm not top brass, McIlwaine. Maybe once. Not now. I blotted my copybook.

MCILWAINE: How?

MILLEN: Should we waken the boys?

MCILWAINE: Give them time to dream. How, Pyper?

PYPER: Just being the black sheep.

MCILWAINE: Bit of a wild one?

PYPER: Bit.

MCILWAINE: Like myself. I broke the mother's heart.

PYPER: I broke my mother's arm. More practical, more painful.

MILLEN: Pyper, how can you laugh at a time like this?

PYPER: I'm not laughing, Millen.

MILLEN: Have you contacts up above there? Ones posted to watch over you and make sure you end up in some cushy corner? Is that why you can laugh?

PYPER: Get something into that thick Coleraine skull of yours, Millen. Nobody's watching over me except myself. What the hell has got into you?

MILLEN: What got into you the first time we met you. Remember? Knowing we're all going to die. Knowing we're all going . . .

(MCILWAINE *grabs* MILLEN.)

MCILWAINE: One minute, you. Just one minute. These chaps are having a well-earned kip. Now they're not going to come to their senses listening to a squealing woman keening after death. Do you hear? If you want to make traitors of them, you'll deal with me first. And if you want out, start marching now.

MILLEN: I've never run away from what I had to do. I commanded –

PYPER: We all know that. But there's more than sixteen-year-old Fenians you're up against now. Will that hit you once and for all?

MCILWAINE: I'm warning you.

PYPER: Let him go, McIlwaine.

MILLEN: I never thought I was a coward.

MCILWAINE: You're not a coward. You've done enough to prove that.

MILLEN: But I'm a soldier.

MCILWAINE: You're a man. The shit's scared out of you. Do you think you're on your own?

MILLEN: No.

MCILWAINE: Well then.

(ROULSTON *wakes up*.)

PYPER: Rise and shine, Christopher.

ROULSTON: Jesus, my mouth feels like a rat's been there.

PYPER: It probably has.

ROULSTON: Did you put it there?

PYPER: There was a time I would have.

ROULSTON: Pleasant as ever.

PYPER: Full of laughs.

ROULSTON: Any word?

MILLEN: Nothing new.

ROULSTON: I suppose they're saying the same thing over there?

MCILWAINE: In German?

PYPER: No, in Gaelic.

MCILWAINE: Germans don't speak Gaelic.

PYPER: They all learn it for badness, McIlwaine.

MCILWAINE: Dirty bastard. So that's what they insult you in.

PYPER: Couldn't watch them. Fenians, Gaelic speakers. They get everywhere. Even in the German army.

MCILWAINE: No way. Not even the Germans would have them. Did you hear about this boy Pearse? The boy who took over a post office because he was short of a few stamps.

MILLEN: He did more than take over a post office, the bastard. Shot down our men until he got what he was looking for.

MCILWAINE: Let me finish. He was a Fenian, wasn't he? No soldier. He took over this big post office in Dublin, kicks all the wee girls serving behind the counter out on to the streets. When the place is empty, him and his merry men all carrying wooden rifles, land outside on the street. Your

64

man reads the proclamation of an Irish republic. The Irish couldn't spell republic, let alone proclaim it. Then he's caught, him and all hands in gaol. He starts to cry, saying he has a widowed mother and he had led the only other brother astray. Anyway, he didn't plan to take over this post office. He walked in to post a letter and got carried away and thought it was Christmas. Nobody believes him. They're leading him out to be shot. He's supposed to see the widowed ma in the crowd. He looks at her and says, pray for me, mother. The ma looks back at him, looks at the Tommy, he's guarding Pearse, the old one grabs the Tommy's rifle. She shoots Pearse herself. She turns to the Tommy and she says, 'That'll learn him, the cheeky pup. Going about robbing post offices. Honest to God, I'm affronted.' So you see, Fenians can't fight. Not unless they're in a post office or a bakery or a woman's clothes shop. Disgrace to their sex, the whole bastarding lot of them, I say.

PYPER: Who gave you this version of events?

MCILWAINE: Christopher here.

PYPER: Roulston?

ROULSTON: He invented quite a few details of his own. The best ones.

MCILWAINE: I can't help that. I'm very imaginative. I play the drums, you see. An artist like yourself, Pyper. We're a breed apart, us boys. To hell with the truth as long as it rhymes.

ROULSTON: How's Johnny?

MILLEN: All right, Roulston.

ROULSTON: You're keeping up?

MILLEN: Why shouldn't I be?

ROULSTON: That's the spirit.

MILLEN: Spirit?

MCILWAINE: Thanks, I'll have a double whiskey. Bushmills, if you have it. If not, anything goes. Have one yourself. It'll liven you up.

MILLEN: Doesn't take much to liven you up.

MCILWAINE: No, not much. Then again, there mightn't be

many more chances to be livened up. Don't forget that.

MILLEN: I'm hardly liable –

PYPER: All right, enough. Do something with yourself, Millen.
Check your stuff, do anything, just keep busy.

MILLEN: Pyper, do you think I have not tried?

MCILWAINE: I've warned you before –

MILLEN: I've warned myself often enough before and I cannot –

ROULSTON: Johnny, God's good. He's looked after us up to
now. He's with us. He won't desert us.

MILLEN: He deserted us when he led us here.

PYPER: We led ourselves here.

ROULSTON: Pyper, leave him. Would it help you if we prayed
together, Johnny?
(*Silence.*)

PYPER: You heard the man, Millen.

MILLEN: It might, I haven't prayed for a long time –

ROULSTON: Neither have I. Together?

MILLEN: What? Pray what? What kind of prayer?

ROULSTON (*Sings:*)
From depths of woe I raise to thee
The voice of lamentation.
Lord, turn a gracious ear to me
And hear my supplication.
If thou shouldst be extreme to mark
Each secret sin and misdeed dark
Oh! Who could stand before Thee!

(MILLEN *joins in the hymn:*)
To wash away the crimson stain
Grace, grace alone availeth.
Our works alas are all in vain
In much the best life faileth.
No man can glory in Thy sight,
All must alike confess Thy might,
And live alone by mercy.

(MCILWAINE *begins to sing:*)
Therefore my trust is in the Lord
And not in my own merit
On Him my soul shall rest, His word

Upholds my fainting spirit.
His promised mercy is my fort,
My comfort and my sweet support.
I wait for it in patience.
(*Silence.*)

PYPER: Patience. I'm growing tired of waiting. Let it come.
(CRAIG *cries out in his sleep.*)
David?
(*Silence.*)
Sleep.

ROULSTON: Maybe you should get a bit of rest, Millen.

MILLEN: No point. Soon have to move.

MCILWAINE: Nice tune to that one, wasn't there? I could never remember words, but I never forgot a tune in my life.

ROULSTON: You're speaking in the past tense.

MCILWAINE: What?

ROULSTON: Nothing.

MILLEN: I never recall it as quiet as this.

MCILWAINE: The smell's different today. Has anybody noticed? Or am I imagining things?
(CRAWFORD *wakes up.*)

PYPER: No, there's something different in the air.

ROULSTON: Stronger.

MCILWAINE: What is it?

MILLEN: Fear.

ROULSTON: Are you awake?

CRAWFORD: Just about.

ROULSTON: Cold?

CRAWFORD: Ice. I'm still tired. Christ, I'm eaten by lice. Give us a scratch.
(ROULSTON *puts his hand down* CRAWFORD's *shirt.*)
Good man, lovely. Down to the left a bit.

MCILWAINE: Want some powder?

CRAWFORD: Useless bloody stuff. We're still here?

MCILWAINE: No, we're on our way to Bangor for a bathe.

CRAWFORD: Don't tear the face off me. I was only asking.

ROULSTON: You slept all right?

CRAWFORD: All right. Up long?

ROULSTON: A while.

CRAWFORD: That's enough. Is there time for a quick match?

MCILWAINE: You have the football with you?

PYPER: I have to hand it to your nerve, Crawford.

CRAWFORD: Have to practice, man. Any time, anywhere. I want to get into the game seriously when I'm home again. Come on. A quick game.

MILLEN: Not yet.

CRAWFORD: Liven you up.

MCILWAINE: Right. I'm your man.

(CRAWFORD *starts the game.* ANDERSON *wakes up. The game continues through the following dialogue.*)

Would you like some breakfast, son?

ANDERSON: Fried egg, bit of bacon, sausages?

MCILWAINE: Soda faral.

ANDERSON: Strong tea?

MCILWAINE: Name your poison.

ANDERSON: Aye, wouldn't mind.

MCILWAINE: Sorry, haven't got it.

ANDERSON: What have you got?

MCILWAINE: Bit of shite.

ANDERSON: Horse's?

MCILWAINE: Are you mad? Can't get horse's shite for love or money.

ANDERSON: Only human?

MCILWAINE: Aye.

ANDERSON: No thanks.

MCILWAINE: Don't turn up your nose at it. It'll soon be scarce enough.

ANDERSON: Not when your mouth's still around.

MCILWAINE: Compliments flying.

ANDERSON: So's the shite.

CRAWFORD: Yous two are pretty sharp.

MCILWAINE: Lethal, son, lethal.

ANDERSON: We practise in the dark.

CRAWFORD: Did yous ever think of taking it up full time?

ANDERSON: Good idea.

MCILWAINE: What would we do?

ANDERSON: Any suggestions?

PYPER: Something sad.

ANDERSON: Damn sadness. Something to make the blood boil.

MCILWAINE: Battle of the Boyne?

ANDERSON: How the hell can two men do the Battle of the Boyne?

MCILWAINE: They do it without much more at Scarva.

ANDERSON: Very thing, Battle of Scarva.

MCILWAINE: They have horses at Scarva.

ANDERSON: We'll get the horses. To your feet, Millen. You're a horse.

MILLEN: Let me be.

ANDERSON: Get him to his feet.

(MCILWAINE *hauls* MILLEN *to his feet.*)

Now, Pyper, you're the blondie boy. King Billy at Scarva always has a white horse. You're his horse, right? Now for King Billy. Who could Pyper carry? Crawford. You, on his shoulders. Right?

CRAWFORD: Wait a minute –

ANDERSON: Do as you're told.

ROULSTON: Come on, King Billy.

(CRAWFORD *gets on* PYPER's *shoulders.* PYPER *neighs loudly.*)

ANDERSON: Raring to go. King Billy and his trusty white steed. Now Millen, you're King James's horse. Who could you carry?

MILLEN: I'm having no part in this.

ANDERSON: Could you carry me?

MILLEN: Go to hell.

MCILWAINE: Waken Craig.

MILLEN: Craig's like a horse himself.

MCILWAINE: Moore then.

ANDERSON: Get up, Moore.

MOORE: What's wrong?

MCILWAINE: You're King James. Get on –

MOORE: I'm what?

MCILWAINE: King James. Get on Millen's shoulders.

MILLEN: I have no part in this.

69

MOORE: Part in what?

ANDERSON: Battle of Scarva. Come on, get on.

(ANDERSON *and* MCILWAINE *lift* MOORE *on to* MILLEN's *shoulders*.)

MILLEN: Why do we have to be King James? He has to get beaten.

MCILWAINE: Because somebody has to be King James. And anyway, you're only his horse.

MILLEN: This is not a fair fight.

ANDERSON: What fight ever is fair? Are yous right? Let battle commence. And remember, King James, we know the result, you know the result, keep to the result.

(*The Mock Battle of Scarva begins*.)

Music.

MCILWAINE: How can we have music? Sing a hymn?

ANDERSON: Lilt or something. Go on, lilt.

ROULSTON: Lilt?

MCILWAINE: Lilt.

(*They lilt*.)

ANDERSON: King William, Prince of Orange, on his fine white charger eyes the traitor James, James who will destroy our glorious religion should he win the battle. William moves defiantly towards the bitter enemy. His white steed sniffs the dangers but continues to carry his master to glory. James swaggers forward –

MILLEN: On his trusty steed –

ANDERSON: Will his trusty steed shut his mouth when I'm in the middle of the story? Where was I? James swaggers forward, his Papist pride on high. No one shall topple the favoured son of Rome. But look at how King William –

ROULSTON: Come on, King William.

MCILWAINE: He's going to win anyway. Just lilt.

ANDERSON: Look at how King William, brandishing his golden blade, defies the might of haughty James, minion of Rome. They pass in thick of battle. But the wily James avoids the first attack. Behold, undaunted, our King returns, the loyal steed beneath him devours the ground. This time for the traitor James there is no escape. But luck is on the devil's

70

side. James has swerved in time. Furious and bold, King
Billy will not rest. This time James will fall, and with him
mighty Rome in this kingdom. They must fight and fight
they will until the victor stands poised before the victim –
(PYPER *trips.* CRAWFORD *crashes to the ground. Silence.*
MILLEN *lets* MOORE *off his shoulders.* ROULSTON *and*
MOORE *help* CRAWFORD *to rise.* PYPER *lies on the ground.*)

MOORE: Can you manage?

ROULSTON: He's just a bit stunned.

ANDERSON: Get up, Pyper.

PYPER: I fell.

MCILWAINE: We saw.

MILLEN: Not the best of signs.

(*Silence.*)

CRAWFORD: It was as much my fault as Pyper's. I lost control
of his shoulders. That's what happened.

ROULSTON: You're all right?

CRAWFORD: I'm grand.

MILLEN: Day's breaking.

MOORE: Is everybody ready?

PYPER: Better waken Craig.

ANDERSON: Better waken yourself, Pyper. Why did you do that?

PYPER: I just fell.

ANDERSON: Did you?

CRAWFORD: It's not only his fault.

MCILWAINE: Let it rest. It was only a game.

ROULSTON: Good sport while it lasted.

ANDERSON: Great. Fair great.

MOORE: Prepare us for the real thing.

ROULSTON: Yes, it's coming. Better prepare.

CRAWFORD: Were yous talking about a smell when I woke up?

MCILWAINE: Aye, why?

CRAWFORD: I find it now. What is it?

ROULSTON: The smell's always there.

CRAWFORD: But this is like, this is like –

MILLEN: What?

CRAWFORD: I don't know.

MILLEN: I noticed how quiet it was too.

71

PYPER: David, get up.

MILLEN: Did anyone else?

CRAWFORD: We were making that much noise, no.

PYPER: Come on, man, rise.

CRAIG: What? Are we off?

PYPER: Nearly.

CRAIG: Orders come?

PYPER: We're waiting for it. It's almost daylight.

CRAIG: Oh God. Right.

MOORE: How did you sleep through all the din, man?

CRAIG: What din?

MOORE: You must have been dead to the world.

CRAIG: I had this dream. A very clear dream.

MOORE: A nightmare?

CRAIG: No, no. Good. Very good.

MCILWAINE: What about?

CRAIG: Home.

ROULSTON: Enniskillen?

CRAIG: Yes.

MOORE: 'Fare thee well, Enniskillen.'

CRAIG: 'Fare thee well for a time.'

PYPER: (*Sings:*)

> And all around the borders of Erin's green isle.
> And when the war is over we'll return in fine bloom
> And we'll all welcome home our Enniskillen dragoons.

CRAIG: 'Fare thee well, Enniskillen.'

PYPER: 'Fare thee well for a while.'

CRAIG: Lough Erne.

MOORE: Good weather there at the minute.

MCILWAINE: How would you know?

MOORE: Letters. Great weather all over. The Bann's fair jumping with salmon at the minute.

MILLEN: Nobody to catch them.

MOORE: Young lads might.

MILLEN: They ruin a river.

CRAIG: They never know when to stop.

MILLEN: I threw back more fish than I ever ate.

CRAIG: I didn't know you were much of a fisherman.

72

MOORE: Oh aye. The two of us. In the summer the banks of the Bann are a second home.

PYPER: Beautiful rivers.

MILLEN: The loveliest, and say what you like, Coleraine's at its best point.

CRAWFORD: Foyle.

CRAIG: What?

CRAWFORD: I'm just remembering the Foyle. I'd forgotten it. Reared by it. Foyle Street.

MCILWAINE: Well, the Lagan isn't bad either.

MOORE: Nobody said it was.

MCILWAINE: It could knock the bloody Erne into the shade any day. And as for the Bann, I wouldn't make my water into it in case it would flood.

MOORE: Wait one minute. Let me tell you –

PYPER: Keep it easy.

(*Silence.*)

Jesus, that's it. The source of the strange smell. The river.

ROULSTON: The Somme?

PYPER: The Somme.

CRAWFORD: How? It's far –

PYPER: It carries for miles. It smells like home. A river at home.

ANDERSON: All rivers smell the same.

PYPER: Not your own river.

MCILWAINE: I've never smelt a river.

PYPER: You can't stop smelling a river. Anyway, do you not see why it's started to change smell?

ANDERSON: What's that man on about?

PYPER: It's bringing us home. We're not in France. We're home. We're on our own territory. We're fighting for home. This river is ours. This land's ours. We've come home. Where's Belfast, Anderson?

ANDERSON: You know as well as I do where –

PYPER: It's out there. It's waiting for you. Can you hear the shipyard, McIlwaine?

MCILWAINE: Your head's cut, man.

PYPER: You weren't dreaming about Lough Erne, David.

You're on it. It surrounds you. Moore, the Bann is flowing outside. The Somme, it's not what we think it is. It's the Lagan, the Foyle, the Bann –

CRAIG: You're trying too hard, Pyper. It's too late to tell us what we're fighting for. We know where we are. We know what we've to do. And we know what we're doing it for. We knew before we enlisted. We joined up willingly for that reason. Everyone of us, except you. You've learned it at long last. But you can't teach us what we already know. You won't save us, you won't save yourself, imagining things. There's nothing imaginary about this, Kenneth. This is the last battle. We're going out to die.

PYPER: No, David, you –

CRAIG: Yes, yes. Whoever comes back alive, if any of us do, will have died as well. He'll never be the same. Different men after this, one way or the other. Do you know why we'll risk going through that? Because we want to.

MILLEN: None of us want to die.

CRAIG: I said even to come through this will be the same as dying.

MCILWAINE: How do you know it's going to be that bad?

CRAIG: The gods told me.

ROULSTON: What did they tell?

CRAIG: The Protestant gods told me. In a dream. On Lough Erne. Get yourselves ready. Make your peace with God and man.

(*The men divide slowly into the pairings of part 3.*)

ANDERSON: What's got into your man Craig?

MCILWAINE: Sense.

ANDERSON: He's been hanging around too long near Pyper.

MCILWAINE: Has he?

ANDERSON: Did you hear that silly chat about rivers?

MCILWAINE: There's more there than you think.

ANDERSON: I know what I think. That man Pyper's a lunatic.

MCILWAINE: Remember that night on the Field you thought he was thinking right?

ANDERSON: No.

MCILWAINE: Good.

74

ANDERSON: What's got into you?

MCILWAINE: Maybe I've got sense as well. All right?

ANDERSON: Hi, I'm sorry.

MCILWAINE: What for?

ANDERSON: I don't know what's going to happen.

MCILWAINE: You do, Anderson. You do.

MOORE: Are you feeling any better?

MILLEN: Willy, I lied to you. I lied to you all my life. Was it you or me lost their nerve? Who crossed the bridge?

MOORE: We did together.

MILLEN: I couldn't have done it.

MOORE: You have to save yourself today, Johnny, you can't save me. We're on our own today.

MILLEN: You think like Craig we're not coming back?

MOORE: What do you think?

MILLEN: That it's over.

MOORE: Go down fighting.

MILLEN: Take me back.

MOORE: Where?

MILLEN: Home.

MOORE: This is home.

MILLEN: Death?

MOORE: You have to look it in the face. Watch yourself.

MILLEN: I need you.

MOORE: I'm beside you.

MILLEN: Then we'll sink together.

MOORE: Or swim.

MILLEN: Or swim.

(MOORE *and* MILLEN *shake hands*.)

CRAWFORD: It's different to what I thought.

ROULSTON: How?

CRAWFORD: Quieter.

ROULSTON: What's done has to be done.

CRAWFORD: I thought when this day come you'd have been angrier.

ROULSTON: With you?

CRAWFORD: How with me? I meant with God.

ROULSTON: I'm not sure I can tell the difference any more.

75

Anyway, it was always leading to this.

CRAWFORD: Don't say that.

ROULSTON: Why not?

CRAWFORD: Cowardly.

ROULSTON: Is that not what I am?

CRAWFORD: You've proved yourself before. You'll do it today as well.

ROULSTON: Proved what? That I can handle a gun? Stick a bayonet where it's needed? Am as good a man as any soldier? That proves nothing. What you said about me in the church that day was the truth. It was shown to me. You showed me. I accept it. No better and no worse than any of you. None of us are.

CRAWFORD: Do you still believe?

ROULSTON: Yes.

CRAWFORD: Would you do me a favour?

ROULSTON: What?

CRAWFORD: Pray I'll come back.

ROULSTON: No.

CRAWFORD: Why not?

ROULSTON: You can do that for yourself. Do it now.

CRAWFORD: Do it with me then.

ROULSTON: Wait till the word's given to go.

CRAIG: I'm sorry.

PYPER: Why did you do that?

CRAIG: To stop the heroism.

PYPER: I wasn't –

CRAIG: You were being stupid. We could do without that, you know.

PYPER: Why are you changing?

CRAIG: Because you're going back. You'll go back to your proud family. The brave eldest son. Made a man of himself in Flanders. Damn you, after listening to that bit of rabble-rousing, I saw through you. You're wasted here with us. You're not of us, man. You're a leader. You got what you wanted. You always have, you always will. You'll come through today because you learned to want it.

PYPER: I've learned to want you.

CRAIG: No. Tell me this. What kind of life do you see for us when we're out of here? It might be many things, but it won't be together.

PYPER: What do you want from me?

CRAIG: What you want.

PYPER: I don't understand you.

CRAIG: No. You don't. For the first time, and that's good. I'm your measure. Don't forget that.

PYPER: Stop this.

CRAIG: If I'm hurting you, it's about time.

PYPER: Don't go out like this.

CRAIG: It's the way I need to go out 'nere. Kenneth, don't die. One of us has to go on.

PYPER: David –

CRAIG: Calm.

PYPER: Home.

CRAIG: Here.

ANDERSON: Hi, Pyper?

PYPER: What do you want?

ANDERSON: We've noticed something missing from your uniform. Something important. We think you should do something about it. It might get you into trouble.

PYPER: What's missing?

ANDERSON: Your badge of honour.

(ANDERSON *hands out an Orange sash to* PYPER.)
Well?

PYPER: It's not mine.

ANDERSON: It is now. It's a gift. From us. Am I right, McIlwaine?

MCILWAINE: Right. Very right. Damned right. Anderson gets sensible when he's right, Pyper.

(*Silence.*)

ANDERSON: Will you wear it this time, like the rest of us?

PYPER: Why?

ANDERSON: So we'll recognize you as one of our own. Your own.

PYPER: We're on the same side.

ANDERSON: I'm sure we are. Here, take it.

(*Silence.*)

77

I said take it. Do you want me to put it round you?
(PYPER *snatches the sash.*)
That's the man. That's the way.
CRAWFORD: Are you ready, Roulston?
MOORE: What for?
CRAWFORD: The last prayer.
ROULSTON: Together.
ALL (*Sing*)
> I'm but a stranger here,
> Heaven is my home.
> Earth is but a desert drear,
> Heaven is my home.
> Danger and sorrow stand
> Round me on every hand.
> Heaven is my fatherland,
> Heaven is my home.
>
> What though the tempest rage,
> Heaven is my home.
> Short is my pilgrimage,
> Heaven is my home.
> Time's wild and wintry blast
> Soon will be overpast.
> I shall reach home at last.
> Heaven is my home.
>
> There at my Saviour's side –
> Heaven is my home –
> I shall be glorified,
> Heaven is my home.
> There are the good and blest,
> Those I love most and best,
> And there I too shall rest.
> Heaven is my home.
>
> Therefore I murmur not,
> Heaven is my home.
> Whate'er my earthly lot,

Heaven is my home.
And I shall surely stand
There at the Lord's right hand.
Heaven is my fatherland,
Heaven is my home.

MOORE: I can see the others gathering.

MILLEN: It's time then.

MCILWAINE: All together.

CRAWFORD: Better move.

ROULSTON: Every one.

CRAIG: Right.

ANDERSON: Last stage.

(*With the exception of* PYPER, *they each begin to put on their Orange sashes.* CRAIG *watches* PYPER, *then takes his sash off, goes to* MOORE, *hands it to him.* MOORE *hesitates, then exchanges his sash for* CRAIG's. *At this there is an exchange of sashes,* CRAWFORD's *for* ANDERSON's, MILLEN's *for* MCILWAINE's. ROULSTON *goes to* PYPER, *who takes* ROULSTON's *and gives him his own.*)

PYPER: It's come to this, Roulston?

ROULSTON: What's decreed passes, Pyper.

PYPER: There's no fight back?

ROULSTON: There's just the fight.

PYPER: The good fight?

ROULSTON: The everlasting fight.

PYPER: Inside us?

ROULSTON: And outside us.

PYPER: Preach.

ROULSTON: No. You preach.

(*Silence. They wait.*)

You believe. Believe.

(*Silence.*)

PYPER: God in heaven, if you hear the words of man, I speak to you this day. I do it now to ask we be spared. I do it to ask for strength. Strength for these men around me, strength for myself. If you are a just and merciful God, show your mercy this day. Save us. Save our country. Destroy our enemies at home and on this field of battle. Let this day at the Somme be as glorious in the memory of Ulster as that day at the Boyne, when you scattered our enemies. Lead us back from this exile. To Derry, to the Foyle. To Belfast and the Lagan. To Armagh. To Tyrone. To the Bann and its banks. To Erne and its islands. Protect them. Protect us. Protect me. Let us fight bravely. Let us win gloriously. Lord, look down on us. Spare us. I love – . Observe the sons of Ulster marching towards the Somme. I love their lives. I love my own life. I love my home. I love my Ulster. Ulster. Ulster. Ulster. Ulster. Ulster. Ulster. Ulster. Ulster. (*As the chant of 'Ulster' commences rifles and bayonets are raised. The chant turns into a battle cry, reaching frenzy. The* ELDER PYPER *appears. His* YOUNGER SELF *sees him. The chant ceases.*)

YOUNGER PYPER: Ulster.

ELDER PYPER: Ulster.

YOUNGER PYPER: I have seen horror.

ELDER PYPER: Ulster.

YOUNGER PYPER: They kept their nerve, and they died.

ELDER PYPER: Ulster.

YOUNGER PYPER: There would be, and there will be, no surrender.

ELDER PYPER: Ulster.

YOUNGER PYPER: The house has grown cold, the province has grown lonely.

ELDER PYPER: Ulster.

YOUNGER PYPER: You'll always guard Ulster.

ELDER PYPER: Ulster.

YOUNGER PYPER: Save it.

ELDER PYPER: Ulster.

YOUNGER PYPER: The temple of the Lord is ransacked.

ELDER PYPER: Ulster.

(PYPER *reaches towards himself.*)

YOUNGER PYPER: Dance in this deserted temple of the Lord.

ELDER PYPER: Dance.

(*Darkness.*)